Bootstrapping MVC

Using Bootstrap and the MVC Framework
to Build Web Applications

James Chambers

Bootstrapping MVC

Using Bootstrap and the MVC Framework to Build Web Applications

James Chambers

This book is for sale at http://leanpub.com/bootstrappingmvc

This version was published on 2014-08-13

ISBN 978-1-312-41068-8

This is a Leanpub book. Leanpub empowers authors and publishers with the Lean Publishing process. Lean Publishing is the act of publishing an in-progress ebook using lightweight tools and many iterations to get reader feedback, pivot until you have the right book and build traction once you do.

Tweet This Book!

Please help James Chambers by spreading the word about this book on Twitter!

The suggested hashtag for this book is #BootstrappingMvc.

Find out what other people are saying about the book by clicking on this link to search for this hashtag on Twitter:

https://twitter.com/search?q=#BootstrappingMvc

To my beautiful wife, Angie, who has always gone well beyond the mark of supporting, encouraging and tolerating my efforts to learn, share and mentor. She is my rudder and the supplier of strength in our family, an incredible mother to our three mancubs and possibly the best undiscovered celebrity chef in the world.

Contents

Introduction to Bootstrapping Mvc

This book is a series of exercises in which you will see a wide range of topics, tips, tricks. You'll walk through some of the and the ins-and-outs of working with the Bootstrap library and CSS framework with Asp.Net's MVC Framework.

The following chapters will focus on using three key bits that are pre-requisites for the contained exercises: Visual Studio 2013, MVC 5 and Bootstrap. Along the way we're going to make use of jQuery to make the client development a little less mundane.

Experience and Expectations

I'm assuming you're a dev with some web experience, with at least a bit of a handle on how to work around in Visual Studio. You should be fairly fluent in HTML as I won't explain much there, and you should be able to follow along with CSS and JavaScript. I suspect you've heard of the MVC Framework and have either tried some development on your own, or perhaps created a project or two with it, and you're wondering where Bootstrap fits in and how to make it part of your site.

The book is laid out in such a way that you can follow along from the start, creating your own application that demonstrates some of what these frameworks have to offer. My hope is that there is something new for you each day, or at least a new twist on something you might be familiar with. Bring your willingness to try a bit of code, and I'll try to bring some awesome.

This will likely be the least linear book that you'll work through! I learn by doing and don't hesitate to dive in, so I take the same approach when I'm writing about the topics I'd like to share. Expect to parachute down to code level in one chapter then rocket back up to 30,000 feet the next. I believe this is the best way to explore, experiment and learn from the mistakes we make along the way. Remember, software development must be the only profession on the planet where it's okay to be wrong at least 1/3 of the time!

The 30 Day Challenge

Each of these chapters are short by design. If you give yourself 15 minutes each day for 30 days you will be able to complete all the exercises in this book. You will know MVC and Bootstrap better, and you'll be on your way to building some great apps. The intent here is not to make you a better programmer, but to enable you to program better by exposing you to the inner bits that make these two frameworks such great compliments to each other.

Warming Up

To start things off we'll have a brief look at the starter project for MVC 5, the structure of the solution and learn a little about the intent and benefits of Bootstrap. We'll also dive in a little and explore controllers and actions.

- Chapter 1: The MVC 5 Starter Project
- Chapter 2: Examining the Solution Structure
- Chapter 3: Adding a Controller and View
- Chapter 4: Making a Page Worth a Visit
- Chapter 5: Bootstrap for the Asp.Net Developer

Enhancing Our Views

We don't want to have to do the same thing over and over, so these chapters look at leveraging the MVC Framework to minimize the amount of repetitive tasks in our work.

- Chapter 6: Reusing Design Elements on Multiple Pages
- Chapter 7: Semi-Automatic Bootstrap – Display Templates
- Chapter 8: Semi-Automatic Bootstrap – Editor Templates
- Chapter 9: Templates for Complex Types
- Chapter 10: HtmlHelper Extension Methods
- Chapter 11: Realistic Test Data for Our View

Exploring Bootstrap

Next up, we look at more of what the Bootstrap framework provides and has to offer. We'll look at a couple of the controls, get a better understanding of how the library is structured and even build our own custom version of Bootstrap.

- Chapter 12: Implement Search Using Inline Forms and AJAX
- Chapter 13: Standard Styling and Horizontal Forms
- Chapter 14: Bootstrap Alerts and MVC Framework TempData
- Chapter 15: Some Bootstrap Basics
- Chapter 16: Conceptual Organization of the Bootstrap Library
- Chapter 17: Building Bootstrap in Visual Studio

Adding Some Sparkle

In this section of the book we'll focus more on the MVC Framework side of things and how we can use the building blocks of MVC to more easily create our application.

- Chapter 18: Customizing and Rendering Bootstrap Badges

- Chapter 19: Long-Running Notifications Using Badges and Entity Framework Code First
- Chapter 20: An ActionFilter to Inject Notifications
- Chapter 21: Cleaning Up Filtering, the Layout & the Menu

So, You've Got People Logging In

Giving your visitors a repeatable, personalized experience is only possible once you give them the ability to authenticate. ASP.NET provides some great out-of-box functionality that will help get you setup to handle it, and with Entity Framework to build on from our earlier chapters, you have a scalable platform to build on for storing data.

- Chapter 22: Sprucing up Identity for Logged In Users
- Chapter 23: Choosing Your Own Look-And-Feel
- Chapter 24: Storing User Profile Information
- Chapter 25: Personalizing Notifications
- Chapter 26: Bootstrap Tabs for Managing Accounts
- Chapter 27: Rendering Data in Bootstrap Table

Wrapping Up With Some More Bootstrap

Finally, we're going to take another look at some of the more commonly used controls that are bound to come up on your projects. We'll break them down, see why they work the way they do and add our own, custom behaviors in concert with MVC.

- Chapter 28: Doing More Interesting Things With Buttons
- Chapter 29: Confirmation Dialogs for Delete Actions
- Chapter 30: Loading Bootstrap Modal Content via AJAX

Appendices

Through the development of this content there were some resources that come up, some suggestions and a ton of great questions that came to me through the community. In this eBook-only bonus section, I cover some of these off and point you to resources, more content and code to keep you moving after you're done this book.

As well, if you're looking for a guide on specific topics related to Bootstrap or the MVC Framework be sure to check out Appendix II. This section of the book lets you look for specific aspects of either framework and jump right to the code and content related to those very bits.

- Appendix I: Free Training For All the Peoples!
- Appendix II: The Framework Feature Guide

Following Along with the Source Code

Each chapter of this book builds on the ones before it, so you'll need to have all the code in place in order to complete the exercises. You can either grab the free, completed source for the entire book from the public repository on GitHub, or you can request access to the private repo I maintain with all code for all chapters maintained in separate branches.

Clone or Fork the public Repository on GitHub

This will get you access to the final project, but you may have trouble following along in some of the chapters as we do change things throughout the book. For example, we might add something to a view in an earlier chapter, then move it to a partial later on.

You can visit the GitHub[1] repository to grab the code for the completed project without any need to contact me.

Get Access to the Private Repository

If you didn't get an invite for the private repo when you purchased the book, no worries. Here's what I ask of you to do:

- Follow me on Twitter @CanadianJames[2]

---

[1]https://github.com/MisterJames/BootstrappingMvc-Code
[2]https://twitter.com/CanadianJames

- Tweet "Hey @CanadianJames, can I get access to the #Asp-NetMvc #Bootstrap repository? My GitHub handle is [Put-Your-Handle-Here]."
- If you're not on Twitter, no worries, just send me an email.
- And of course, I hope you buy of copy of this book!

With the private repo I will answer questions, update code, take suggestions for content, make corrections and more.

Checking out Chapter Branches

With a copy of the repository in hand, you can easily switch to any chapter and run the code. This will let you see the completed solution for that chapter.

```
[master]> git checkout chapter-11
[chapter-11]>
```

Switching to a chapter branch

If you're using the excellent GitHub for Windows[3], you'll see that you can just select the branch from the dropdown.

---

[3]https://windows.github.com/

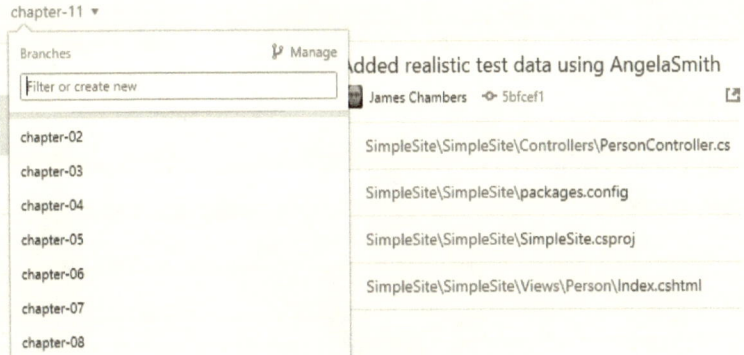

Switching branches in GHfW

 You can always complete an exercise for a chapter by switching to the *previous* chapter branch and continuing from there to follow along. Each chapter branch picks up where the last left off, and every branch represents a completed chapter.

I Warming Up

1. The MVC 5 Starter Project

Getting started in MVC is the easiest it's ever been, and it's even easier to look good doing it. Rather than building up yet another short-lived, likely passing design, Microsoft made another nod to open source software and adopted the Bootstrap library as a design language. We'll get to all those bits shortly, but for now let's see what happens when you get started in MVC 5.

 Estimated time: About 10 minutes

Getting Your Hands a Little Dirty

First off, select File –> New Project from the Visual Studio 2013 menu. If you select the "Web" category you'll see only one type of project, an "Asp.Net Web Application". All web projects have been consolidated under the "One Asp.Net" banner, so the project type is an easy selection. The next dialog that pops up gets a little more interesting:

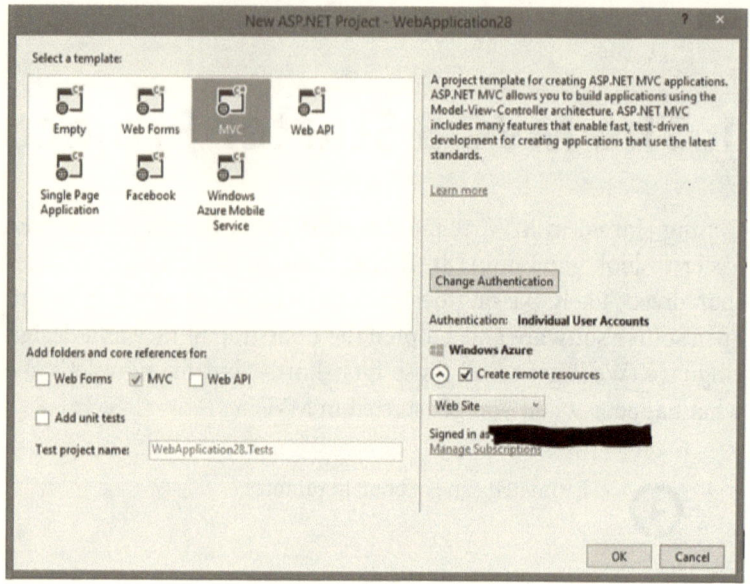

Selecting a project template

You'll note that there are a few more options here. Click around on the project templates to see the description (we're going to be focusing here on MVC). The notable options outside of your template selection are the Authentication, Core References and Azure options.

Authentication - If you're targeting a general web audience you'll likely want to make use of Individual User Accounts (the default), which opens the door for you to integrate with 3rd party providers such as Microsoft, Facebook, Twitter and Google. If this isn't the route for you, click through and read about each of the other types.

Core References - With the removal of project type GUIDs came the arrival of much less hacking to get different types of web projects working in the same solution. You can now easily put Web Forms, MVC and Web API all in the same project. Also here is your ability to add a test project.

Windows Azure - This is the part I like, streamlined deployment baked directly into the project creation. While you can always change these options or even add them later, for those of you who have an Azure account, this is an easy way to get code running quickly in the cloud. If you don't have an account, it's easy to set one up.

Running the Project

Well, don't wait! Just run the site! You'll land on a welcome page (just a static HTML page in your project) but you can hit CTRL+F5 to see your wonderful new digital bits running locally.

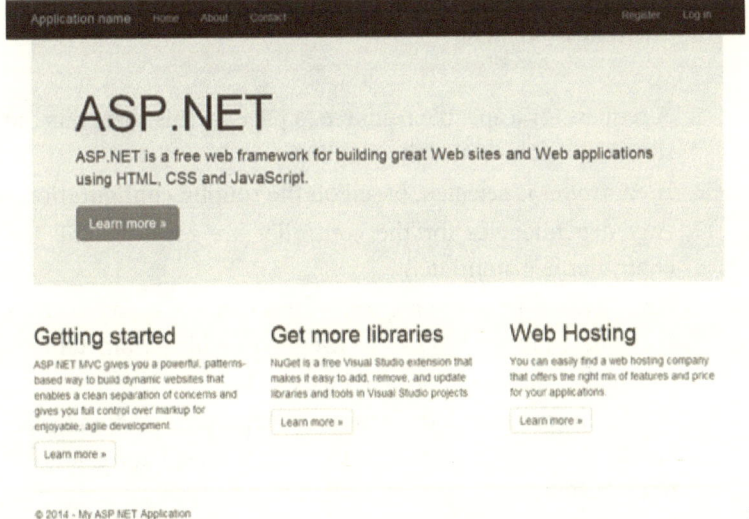

Bang. You got yourself a web site. Let's pause to consider what's going on.

---

[1]http://jameschambers.com/wp-content/uploads/2014/06/image1.png

A Peek Behind the Curtain

Sometimes web development can feel a little bit like magic. Your code might be a mix of c# and Razor markup with no HTML files in the project, yet the page that is delivered to the browser is straight HTML - IMAGE, SCRIPT, P tags and all. The MVC pipeline abstracts away a lot of the dirty bits from the idea of "serving" a page, and relies heavily on the notion that you, as a developer, would rather be writing an application that generates web pages, rather than web pages themselves.

While the detailed discussion over what *actually* happens through-out the lifetime of a request, here's how that content gets rendered to the client in a nutshell:

1. A request for a specific resource (a page, in this case) hits the server and comes into the pipeline.
2. A controller is selected, based on the routing configuration.
3. Any dependencies for the controller are resolved and the controller is instantiated.
4. Any payload from the request - form content, query string - is evaluated to see if it can be used to provide parameters for the method (action) that will be executed.
5. The MVC Framework finds the most appropriate action to call based on the payload and method (POST, GET for example) of the request.
6. The method is invoked, passing in the discovered parameters through a process called model binding.
7. Your code is executed, and you have the option to evaluate and process the incoming data and make a decision about which view the user will see.
8. The information you need (if any) is passed through to Razor, the default view engine.

9. Razor prepares to render the CSHTML file (or VBHTML file) as requested by the framework using anything that was built up so far in the request.

10. Rendering occurs, which often and typically includes a "layout" or master page that is wrapped around the entire content.

11. Happiness ensues. Yay!

Your typical day when building applications on top of the MVC Framework will likely see most of your time spent working in or around steps 7 and 8 from above. While each project has a measure of cruftiness that will need to be built out, you'll find a lot of your time will go into writing actions and views.

There are actually a few more moving parts involved in the request as we'll see in the remaining chapters, and we haven't even talked about application startup yet. The framework also provides a number of ways to intercept requests and participate in the executing pipeline, so we'll cover that as well as the month unfolds.

Chapter 1 Summary

When you have a better idea about the inner workings it's sometimes a little easier to understand what's going on and how to be the most productive. This chapter serves as a basic introduction to the MVC project and the request execution pipeline. From here, you can create, build and run a new MVC-powered website with a little better understanding about the "magic" that goes on behind the scenes.

2. Examining the Solution Structure

Now that we've had a chance to see what the default project looks like when running, let's look at the parts of the project that make it happen. In Chapter 1 we talked briefly about controllers, actions and views, so let's figure out where those come from first before moving on to other important contributors to our project.

 Estimated time: Less than 10 minutes

Controllers and Views, and Actions, Too

One of the things that the MVC Frameworks does reasonably well is to follow convention over configuration. That means that with very little effort you can make use of most of the features of the framework without having to set XML, change project configuration or the like...it just "works" out-of-box. Of course, this means that it is also fairly reasonable to assume that it is somewhat opinionated, especially when it comes to tooling. So, there are "right" ways and "choose your own pain" ways to approach development.

Thankfully, controllers and views are easy pieces, you can find them in the apt-named folders, "Controllers" and "Views", respectfully and consistently across most projects.

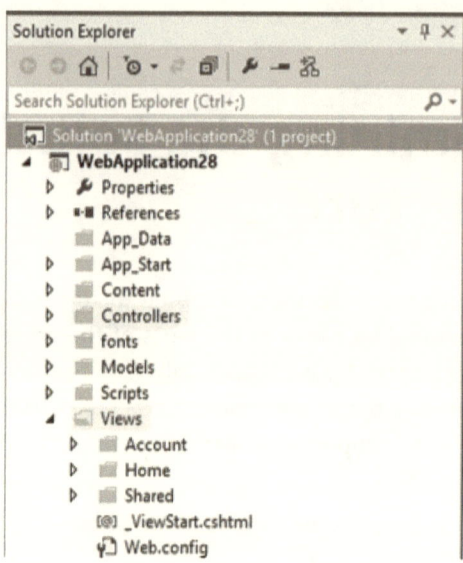

Controllers and Views in the Solution Explorer

Each controller has a corresponding folder inside of Views to help keep things organized further. If you're generating views from the built-in tooling, they are created here as well. As the MVC Framework tries to find the view you would like rendered it checks here first and then falls back to the "shared" folder, also part of convention.

A controller is just a class and actions are just methods. This is an important detail, so keep that in mind as you develop. While you can use either version of either word and be correct, you'll gain the favor of the lexicon if you try to use the terms as they are known in the framework. Other extension points, for example, reference these terms and they are good cues to help other developers (including the future version of you) survive your code down the road.

A view is typically HTML plus some optional code written using the Razor syntax. We don't create "web pages" any more, we create applications. The view engine - Razor - using your view files and any supplied data to assemble and output HTML, which is returned to the client who initiated the request.

Of special note is the Shared folder under Views, where you'll find the layout file (_Layout.cshtml) that is used as a template or "master page" for your site, giving you a way to have pages that follow a similar look-and-feel without having to repeat the same layout instructions on each page.

Models

These guys are pretty easy: they are just classes. Models will have properties and helper methods. They may reflect data that is stored in the database, data that you wish to store in the database, or input from users. They may store options for users to choose from when inputting their data. There are a lot of things Models can be, but for the most part they are just plain old CLR objects (POCOs).

Where things get interesting is when you "pass" a model to a view, allowing an HTML page to be rendered based on the properties of the information contained therein.

Scripts, Content and Fonts

Any web project is driven by a set of static or semi-dynamic resources such as CSS files, images, fonts and JavaScript sources. The solution gives you some basic structure to help keep these organized, but these are not contributors to the MVC project structure and they do not influence the framework. You are free to rename these and organize these types of files as you wish.

The one caveat would be that the default template (mostly driven from your application startup files) does make use of this structure, as do some of the startup components. If you start to move these around, you'll also need to update those aspects of your project.

In these folders you'll find the requisite pieces needed to ship a web site that reflects the Bootstrap design language, namely jQuery, the Bootstrap library and stylesheet, the glyphicons font and a few libraries to assist with browser incompatibilities and functionality polyfills to add capabilities that are missing in out-of-date or non-compliant browsers.

Application Building Blocks

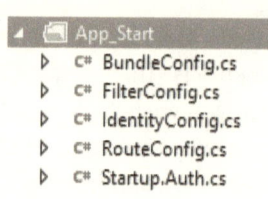

The App_Start Directory

The App_Start folder is likely the most interesting from a code perspective as it provides the wiring to pull your application together. Bundles are a way to reduce and compress script and style resources in a non-lossy fashion (as far as the browser is concerned). Filters allow you to modify the execution pipeline of your application. Identity is the implementation of the built-in local user account manager. Routing allows friendly URLs and custom mapping of resources. And the Startup.Auth file (a partial class) is used to tell your app which types of user identities you'll be using to pair with your local user accounts.

There's a lot in that last little paragraph, but we'll unpack it as we progress through the remaining chapters.

The Root of all Web

We wouldn't be complete if we didn't cover all the bits, including those in the root of our application.

At the top of the solution explorer you'll see "Properties" and "References", standard in all .Net applications. These give you access to things like assembly information, the built-in web server configuration and references to external dependencies that you take.

Towards the bottom of the list you'll see a couple of files that are common on all Asp.Net sites, Global.asax and Web.Config. These give instructions to the MVC Framework, to the Asp.Net runtimes and to IIS itself as to how to execute requests and make use of resources. They allow you to store settings and provide values to libraries and assemblies you might be using. You'll note that Global's startup method calls out to some of the startup classes we covered in the last section as well.

```
AreaRegistration.RegisterAllAreas();
FilterConfig.RegisterGlobalFilters(GlobalFilters.Filters);
RouteConfig.RegisterRoutes(RouteTable.Routes);
BundleConfig.RegisterBundles(BundleTable.Bundles);
```

Methods in the application startup

Favicon.ico is the image that will be displayed in a browser tab when someone visits your site.

Packages.config is a list of all the packages that are required by your application. If you open a project and do not have these packages installed, Visual Studio will go and fetch them for you when you try to build.

There's one last class in there, a file named Startup.cs, which configures the authentication bits via a call to the Configure method in our Startup.Auth partial class. This one is interesting because it leverages an OwinStartupAttribute to get invoked before much else in our app is executed.

Chapter 2 Summary

This chapter talked about how MVC works conceptually and explains some of the basic conventions in use that will make your development easier as you go. It also gave you a better look at how the MVC Framework comes together on the file system and how some of the files in your project interact.

3. Adding a Controller and View

When we talk about "adding a page" to a site, what we usually are referring to is setting up some kind of response to a client request. Sometimes that request will be an HTML page, but it might be a dynamically created image, a file built on the fly, or any other HTTP compliant result.

In any case, if the goal is to try to render something that the user is going to see on their screen, we're likely talking about adding controllers and views.

 Estimated time: About 10 minutes

Creating Controllers

As we already discussed, we will follow the opinions and conventions of the MVC Framework that we might be able to leverage the built in tooling. That means that controllers we create will go in the Controllers folder.

To get started, right-click on the Controllers folder in the solution explorer and follow the context menu to "Add –> Controller...". This is the process for using the scaffolding exposed by the framework, launching a dialog that prompts you for the information it needs to build out a starting point. There are a number of options, but let's just look at first one for now: the Empty Controller.

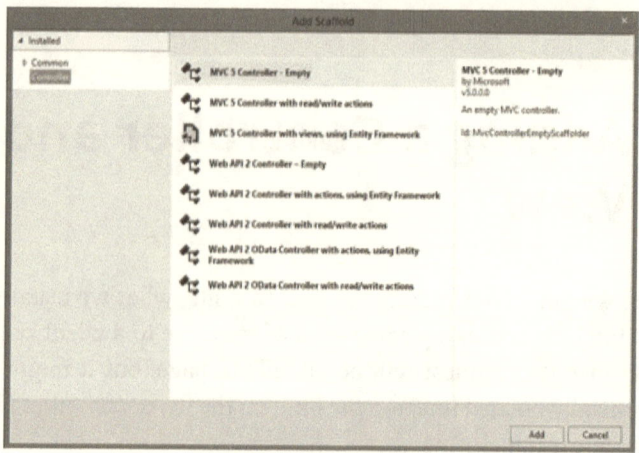

Selecting a Template

This gives you a simple option to name a controller when selected.

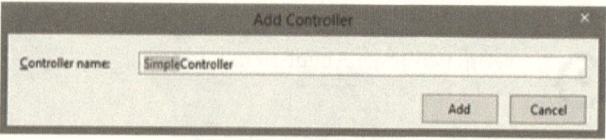

Naming the Controller

I called mine SimpleController, which you'll see has some signifi-
cance in a moment. I don't mean to over-play this convention thing,
but as a class named SimpleController future James will know
exactly what present James meant by this name. Here's the class
that is generated for me.

```
1   public class SimpleController : Controller
2   {
3       // GET: Simple
4       public ActionResult Index()
5       {
6           return View();
7       }
8   }
```

So, again, this is a class with a method, but we call it a controller with an action. In this case, my Index "action" returns the result of a call to the **View** method, which is found on my base class that I inherit from (Controller). **ActionResult**, the return type of **Index**, is a type located in the MVC Framework that we'll look Because we're following convention, the **View** method will attempt to locate a view named "Index" found in the Views folder, in the Simple subfolder.

Unfortunately, that view doesn't yet exist. Thankfully, this isn't hard to do.

Creating Views

In the code editor window, right-click on the Index method (right on the name of the method itself) to invoke the context menu. Select "Add View…" to get the dialog open to create your view.

Scaffolding a View

The nice thing here is that you don't have to type in the name of your view. The tooling just assumes the name from the method.

At this point, use the "Empty" template to create your view and select the option to "Use a layout page" as I have above. Leave the name as-is so that we can follow along on that convention gravy train. When you click "Add", a view file will be created for you with the cshtml (or vbhtml) extension, with something similar to the following code:

```
1  @{
2      ViewBag.Title = "Index";
3  }
4
5  <h2>Index</h2>
```

The @{ ... } notation is Razor syntax to say, "here's a code block". This is used to interact with the rendering of the view programmatically by flipping into code mode, and in this case it's simply setting the value of the page Title in the ViewBag.

With your cursor in the Razor editor, run your application by pressing CTRL+F5 (run without debugger), and navigate to your newly created page. For me, my application started up on port 48995 and the full URL was **http://localhost:48995/Simple/Index**[1]. You can think of that address as **http://host/Controller/View** for any page that is following the default convention for routing.

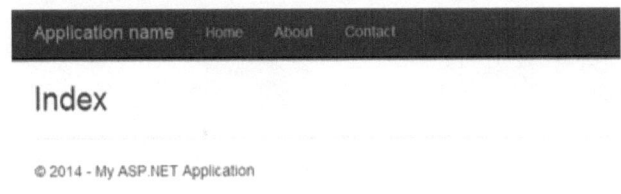

New Page For The Win

You can actually play with this page all you like now, adding whatever HTML you like. Razor is crazy-good at determining which parts of your view are HTML and which parts are code, even when it's not as straightforward as it is above with an explicit code block.

> My controller was named `SimpleController` and my action was named `Index`, so by convention you could just put **http://host/Simple** into the browser (where 'host' is the name and port where the site is running on your machine) and it would work, even without specifying the action. You can examine the mechanics of this further in the App_-Start\RouteConfig.cs class, where defaults are wired up, but where you are also free to choose new defaults or add other routes to your project.

Chapter 3 Summary

This chapter walked you through the processing of creating some new content using the MVC Framework by adding a controller and

---

[1]http://localhost:48995/Simple/Index

the related view to your project. To do this, you used the built-in tooling to scaffold the new files, and ended up with a view that could contain code or HTML to be processed and rendered for the client.

4. Making a Page Worth a Visit

A page instantly becomes more interesting with useful data and a bit of style. Today we're going to stuff a bit of data into our view and rock it out a little bit with some Bootstrap style.

 Estimated time: About 15 minutes

Introducing Some Data

In Chapter 3 we created a controller called SimpleController with an Index method in it. I'm going to come back to that in a moment, but first we need a class to store our data in. Right-click on the Models folder in the solution and select Add –> Class…, then name it Person from the dialog. Add `FirstName`, `LastName`, `Birthdate`, `LikesMusic` and `Skills` (an `ICollection` of `string`) properties, so it ends up looking like so:

```
1   public class Person
2   {
3       public string FirstName { get; set; }
4       public string LastName { get; set; }
5       public DateTime BirthDate { get; set; }
6       public bool LikesMusic { get; set; }
7       public ICollection<string> Skills { get; set;\
8   }
9   }
```

Those properties should give us some interesting data to look at.

Now, return to your Index method on the SimpleController and update the code to do the following:

```
1   public ActionResult Index()
2   {
3       var person = new Person
4       {
5           FirstName = "Billy Jo",
6           LastName = "McGuffery",
7           BirthDate = new DateTime(1990, 6,1),
8           LikesMusic = true,
9           Skills = new List<string>() { "Math", "Sc\
10  ience", "History" }
11      };
12
13      return View(person);
14  }
```

We are initializing a new Person object and updating the call to View() to pass in the person object.

In previous versions of the MVC Framework and Visual Studio, we used to have to build our solution to get the types available to the tooling, this is no longer the case, allowing for a little less back-and-forth and confusion over missing types in the tooling dialogs. A nice new feature!

Scaffolding a View

Now, as nice as that Index page was that we created in the Simple view folder, it's just got to go! Select it from the Solution Explorer and delete it, then return to your SimpleController code file and create a new view in a similar fashion. This time, however, when you're creating the view, you'll need to select the "Details" template and the "Person" class.

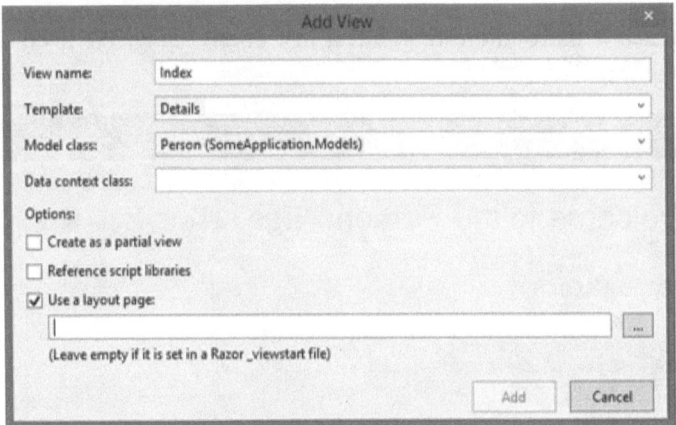

Scaffolding a 'Details' View

Now when you run your application and navigate to Simple/Index, you'll see something like the following:

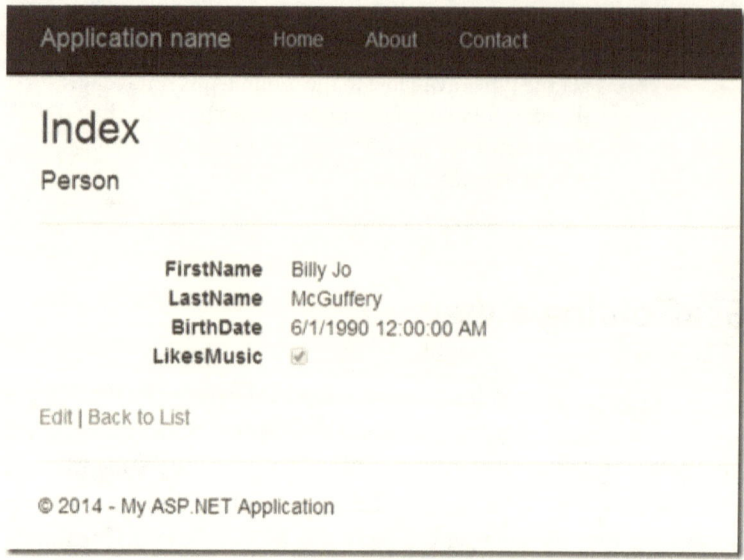

The Default Scaffolded View

...which is more interesting, but it just doesn't sing. We need it to look more like...

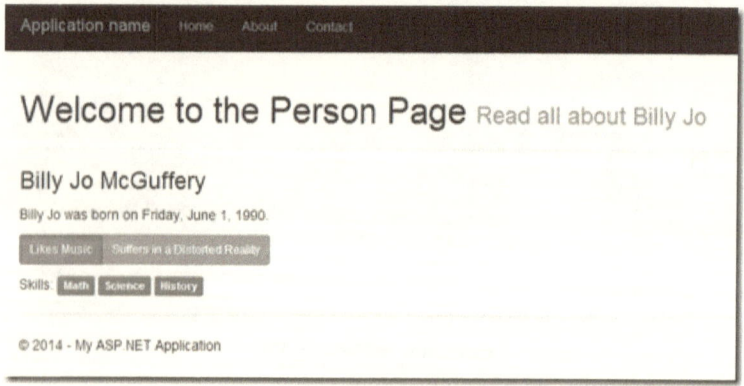

A View With *Zing*!

Bang! Now we're snapping! Let's see how that breaks down.

Bootstrapification

The page is missing some *zing* and some data. So we need to fix that. The scaffolder does its best to drop properties on the page, but it doesn't do so well with collections (without special instructions) and tends to just dump the properties in, more or less, a list. It's a good place to start and helps get a minimal viable product out the door, but it's not pretty.

To get the page looking like version 2 above, there are four main components that we need to address. We'll put these together in order, so these next four code blocks are all sequential. The first is just the setup code for the page, where you set the model type, the page title and collect some information to help render the view.

```
@model SimpleSite.Models.Person

@{
    ViewBag.Title = "Index";
    var likesMusic = Model.LikesMusic ? "active" \
: null;
    var notAMusicFan = !Model.LikesMusic ? "activ\
e" : null;
}
```

Pay at least *some* attention to the namespace in the model name above! If you've named your project differently, you'll need to make sure you bring the fully qualified name of the model in line. Next is three DIVs, each with a slightly different purpose. The first is the page header, a place to block out some info on the page and relay context.

```
1   <div class="page-header">
2       <h1>Welcome to the Person Page <small>Read al\
3   l about @Model.FirstName</small></h1>
4   </div>
```

Then we push out the primary details of the person.

```
1   <div>
2       <h3>@Model.FirstName @Model.LastName</h3>
3       <p>@Model.FirstName was born on @Model.BirthD\
4   ate.ToString("D").</p>
5       <p>
6           <div class="btn-group" data-toggle="butto\
7   ns">
8               <label class="btn btn-success btn-sm \
9   @likesMusic">
10                  <input type="radio" name="options\
11  " id="option1"> Likes Music
12              </label>
13              <label class="btn btn-success btn-sm \
14  @notAMusicFan">
15                  <input type="radio" name="options\
16  " id="option2"> Suffers in a Distorted Reality
17              </label>
18          </div>
19      </p>
20  </div>
```

And finally, we loop through all the skills the person has and set them up as labels.

```
1  <div>
2      <p>
3          Skills:
4          @foreach (var skill in Model.Skills)
5          {
6              <span class="label label-primary">@sk\
7  ill</span>
8          }
9      </p>
10 </div>
```

Chapter 4 Summary

In this chapter we added a model class with some more interesting properties and then used that class to scaffold a new view. We had a look at some basic styling that Bootstrap can offer to spruce up our pages and we used some Razor syntax to output our model.

5. Bootstrap for the Asp.Net Developer

Starting with a blank slate and little direction on where to take things visually is a painful part of web development to overcome, especially for those of us who are in the "design challenged" camp. The Bootstrap[1] front-end framework takes away a lot of the guessing and rework that head-ends most new projects and establishes a design language to work within, while still providing options for look-and-feel via themes.

While we've had a number of options over the years as the Asp.Net templates have evolved, most of them have tended to stick out as visually unappealing and rarely would you let them find their way into production. Today, we have a starting point that marries us to a visual style that we can be happy with publishing.

 Estimated time: Less than 10 minutes

Bootstrap is CSS and JavaScript

You'll include two resources in a page that you want to build off of Bootstrap, the style sheet and the JavaScript library that make it work.

---

[1]http://getbootstrap.com/

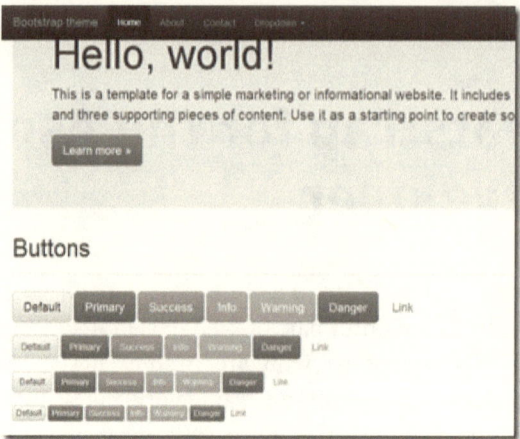

Wham! You got some style!

The CSS aspect gives you a stock option with fonts, colors and components that work well together, a responsive layout grid, and the flexibility to completely modify the framework's default colors, spacing and other variables. You can see how diverse things are at the Bootstrap expo site[2], and build your own theme variant using the tools online[3]. You can also download freely available themes from various sites on the interwebs.

The JavaScript library introduces a number of behaviors and widgets that augment the design with a user experience that most web surfers are now familiar with when working with alerts, tool tips, tabs buttons and more.

Bootstrap is Also Custom HTML Attributes

The next aspect to be aware of is that the framework relies on several custom HTML attributes to kick up the juice. The JavaScript library

---

[2]http://expo.getbootstrap.com/
[3]http://getbootstrap.com/customize/

looks for these attributes to append functionality, help with layout and behaviors and attach events.

```
<body data-spy="scroll" data-target=".navbar-example">
    ...
    <div class="navbar-example">
      <ul class="nav nav-tabs">
          ...
      </ul>
    </div>
    ...
</body>
```
4

The above example, from the docs site, shows how to create a "scroll spy" with no code. Note that all things you can do via attributes can be done with JavaScript as well, so you're not locked into a model.

What I really like about this approach is that the framework isn't as opinionated as, say, jQuery UI about how you must go about your business. The attributes are an easy way to augment your page with minimal code.

Bootstrap is Built In

As of version 5 of the MVC Framework, Microsoft has elected to make Bootstrap the framework of choice in every non-blank web application, making it easy to start working with.

```
bundles.Add(new ScriptBundle("~/bundles/bootstrap").Include(
        "~/Scripts/bootstrap.js",
        "~/Scripts/respond.js"));

bundles.Add(new StyleBundle("~/Content/css").Include(
        "~/Content/bootstrap.css",
        "~/Content/site.css"));
```

The MVC Template Includes The Bootstrap Components

---

[4]http://jameschambers.com/wp-content/uploads/2014/06/image9.png

It's included in the bundles, configured at app startup, and it's included on all child pages that leverage the default layout, located in your Views\Shared folder. Using almost any of the templates, there isn't anything you need to do to include it in your project.

If you do choose to start from the empty template it's still easy to add the layout framework to your project as it's available as a NuGet package. And because it's a versioned package, you'll also be able to upgrade through minor versions of Bootstrap easily enough through the Package Manager Console.

Bootstrap is Actually, Well, Pretty Easy

Once you get your head around the opinions that Bootstrap *does* have, you'll find that creating a toggle button styled in the same way as everything else on your site becomes quite trivial.

```
<div class="btn-group" data-toggle="buttons">
    <label class="btn btn-success btn-sm @likesMusic">
        <input type="radio" name="options" id="option1"> Likes Music
    </label>
    <label class="btn btn-success btn-sm @notAMusicFan">
        <input type="radio" name="options" id="option2"> Suffers in a Distorted Reality
    </label>
</div>
```

Simple Markup Makes the Magic

If we weren't using Bootstrap, we'd still be creating those controls for the radio inputs, and we'd likely have at least one, if not a few, containers to put in place, not to mention the CSS and JavaScript you'd have to write to make it look as you intend...what I'm getting at here is that there's not really much more work to get the benefits of Bootstrap than we'd need to do anyways. And, chances are, our toggle buttons wouldn't behave the same on all browsers, or even look the same without some effort.

Of course, there is more to Bootstrap than just toggle buttons, and there is more to the MVC Framework than spitting out static HTML, so we have some work to do to finish exploring this dynamic duo.

Chapter 5 Summary

Any site you build is going to require at least some knowledge of HTML, CSS and likely JavaScript. This chapter was really about the high-level view of Bootstrap, learning about those aspects of it's design along with the likes of things like custom HTML attributes. We also reviewed how and where it's included in almost every new MVC application by default, as well as through NuGet, making it easy to start using and keep up-to-date.

II Enhancing Our Views

6. Reusing Design Elements on Multiple Pages

While it's important to learn the mechanics of the underlying technology we use, it's never really much fun to have to do the same work over and over again. That's part of why we're here; rather than hacking out the CSS for each site or page, we use frameworks and libraries to bring a uniform look-and-feel.

Likewise, we want to make sure we're leveraging the MVC Framework to do the heavy lifting for us when we're trying to get our data out to the client.

 Estimated time: About 10 minutes

Layouts and Partial Views

In Chapter 2 I briefly mentioned the layout page, located in your Views\Shared directory. This type of "master page" gives you the ability to create a template that can be shared on all pages where you want to wrap your content with common elements, such as side bars, menus, footers and the like, or likewise, to stuff in client-side application scripts, style sheets and other elements.

At the other end of the layout page is the concept of a partial view - a template that can be used to render a specific kind of content in different pages. You may also hear them called by the shortened name of "partials". This allows you to define one time how a set of data will be rendered and then include the partial wherever you need to render the content.

Creating a Partial View

Let's consider for a moment the section of labels that is rendered at
the bottom of our person page that lists the skills.

A List of Strings Rendered as Labels

That block of skills is really just a collection of strings that we
are displaying as labels decorated with Bootstrap styling. I could
imagine that would be handy to have in other places on my site as
well.

Let's look at that code again quickly and see what we have going
on.

```
1   <div>
2       <p>
3           Skills:
4           @foreach (var skill in Model.Skills)
5           {
6               <span class="label label-primary">@sk\
7   ill</span>
8           }
9       </p>
10  </div>
```

Essentially, we're dumping a bunch of SPAN elements to the page
inside of a P tag, all wrapped up in a DIV. Not too complex. There is
a title to describe the list of labels, and a for..each loop that walks
over the collection to dump the labels to the page.

Let's cut that code to the clipboard and paste it into a new file in
the Views\Simple folder called _StringCollection.cshtml. You can

add the file by right-clicking on the Simple folder and selecting Add -> View. When prompted, make sure to tick the "Create as Partial View" so that the scaffolder doesn't set the layout or title, and select the "empty (without model)" template. Using the underscore as a prefix is a convention to let others (and remind yourself) that the file is intended be rendered as a partial view.

Paste the code into the file and update it a little so that the entire partial matches the following code, including the model definition at the top:

```
1   @model ICollection<string>
2
3   <div>
4       <p>
5           @ViewBag.ListDescription
6           @foreach (var value in Model)
7           {
8               <span class="label label-primary">@va\
9   lue</span>
10          }
11      </p>
12  </div>
```

Notice that rather than just writing out "Skills" to the page ahead of our labels, we're now using a property from the ViewBag. Now, return to your Index.cshtml and, in the place of the code that you removed, add the following lines to your view:

```
1  @{
2      ViewBag.ListDescription = "Skills:";
3      Html.RenderPartial("_StringCollection", Model\
4  .Skills);
5  }
```

Run your newly updated page and see...well, you'll see exactly what we had before, but now we're doing it a little more cleverly!

Here we've set the title and then asked Razor, the view engine, to process the partial view file with the contents of the string collection we've passed in. From now on, anywhere in our site, we can push a collection of strings into a label set with a title in two lines of code.

Chapter 6 Summary

Partial views give us a way to wrap up common design elements into reusable templates using the Razor syntax. In this chapter we extracted a visual component of our page and turned it into something that could be included in views or other partial views throughout our site.

7. Semi-Automatic Bootstrap: Using Display Templates

We looked at the idea of using a partial view to make it easier to render certain types of data more easily in Chapter 6. We can go even further, and allow the scaffolder and HTML helpers to render what we're looking for without the need for the additional calls to render partials.

If you provide the MVC Framework with a template to render a type and give the right kind of hints on your class properties you'll be duly rewarded with ease of effort in bringing a rich UI to the client. For now, we'll start with the display end of things.

 Estimated time: About 10 minutes

Bootstrap Styling for Checkboxes

We can really use any type that we want, but I'm going to start with Boolean properties. While they seem at first to be straightforward, they also provide a nullable case that we will need to deal with and render appropriately, much like any other type, yet they're simple enough that we can work through an starter example.

What we're doing here is creating a Display Template. You can think of it as a partial view in a way, but you usually do a bit more to inspect the properties and interact with data from the view engine in order to properly augment the rendering. We'll see more of this in Chapter 8.

Enough chatter...now create a new folder located at Views\Shared\DisplayTemplat and create a file in there called Boolean.cshtml, then paste in the following code:

```
1   @model bool?
2
3   @if (Model.HasValue)
4   {
5       if (Model.Value)
6       { <span class="label label-success">Yes</span\
7   > }
8       else
9       { <span class="label label-warning">No</span>\
10  }
11  }
12  else
13  { <span class="label label-info">Not Set</span> }
```

As the view that is responsible for rendering Boolean values, we must first set the model type of the view. I've used a nullable bool as it's more durable and works with either the basic bool or the nullable version.

The rest of the code is fairly straightforward, just determine if there's a value or not, then set up the label based on the value or lack thereof.

Using the Display Template

Because we named it "Boolean.cshtml", the MVC Framework will use our template in favor of the built-in template for Booleans, which you'll recall from Chapter 4 was simply a checkbox. We saw something like this:

Likes Music:

A Simple Checkbox

But with the new template in place, we'll see this:

Likes Music: Yes

A Great-Looking Way to Represent a Boolean

You can modify your Index.cshtml at this point to see this in action by adding the following line of code:

```
1  <p>Likes Music: @Html.DisplayFor(model => model.L\
2  ikesMusic)</p>
```

And that's it, a call to DisplayFor makes the magic happen. Behind the scenes, the helper method examines the model metadata, determines the correct partial view to use for the type and then renders a string (the HTML that you want) via the Razor view engine. It even takes of of caching the pieces it can for you so that future renders happen without lookups against all the files in your project. From now on, all Boolean values will be rendered as yes/no/not set labels throughout your site.

Chapter 7 Summary

You can create templates that are used to render any type available in your project, including base types from the .Net Framework. Through some clever introspection and with the use of some helper methods you call from your views, the MVC Framework applies the display template for you without any further instructions. Of course, the display is interesting enough, but what about editing? What if you don't want all checkboxes to suffer the same disappearing fate? We'll look at getting the editor in place and to give the MVC Framework more direction on when to use it in Chapter 8.

8. Semi-Automatic Bootstrap: Editor Templates

Now that we have a nice way to consistently display our data, what about editing it? A label is fine to indicate what the saved value is, but it doesn't really solve the issue of input.

 Estimated time: Less than 15 minutes

Introducing Editor Templates

Much in the same way that a shared view can act as the de facto template for rendering data (as we saw in Chapter 7), you can override the default editor output by the framework. Create a new view in Views\Shared\EditorTemplates called Boolean.cshtml and put the following two parts of code in it:

Part 1: Capturing Values to Help Render the Page

```
1    @model bool?
2
3    @{
4        // make use of nullable attribute values
5        var yesSelected = Model.HasValue && Model\
6    .Value ? "active" : null;
7        var noSelected = (Model.HasValue && !Mode\
8    l.Value)
9            || (!Model.HasValue && ViewData.Model\
10   Metadata.IsNullableValueType)
11           ? "active"
12           : null;
13       var noSelection = !Model.HasValue ? "acti\
14   ve" : null;
15
16       // get the name of the ID - this is to su\
17   pport multiple fields
18       var htmlField = ViewData.TemplateInfo.Htm\
19   lFieldPrefix;
20   }
```

As we have in a couple of other places, we're using the "conditional attribute" or "nullable attribute" approach to help us with rendering the desired output on the page. This works by evaluating a field, then either storing a string or a null in the variable. When we add that to the class of an HTML element, as we're doing below, Razor is smart enough to deal with the null. If a null value is the only one we're trying to assign as a CSS class, Razor will even remove the attribute altogether

Now for the rest of the page:

Part 2: The HTML Portion of our Page

```
1    @Html.HiddenFor(model => model)
2
3    <div class="btn-group" data-toggle="buttons">
4        <label class="btn btn-info @yesSelected">
5            <input type="radio" class="bool-@html\
6    Field" onchange="javascript:$('#@htmlField').val(\
7    true);" /> Yes
8        </label>
9        <label class="btn btn-info @noSelected">
10           <input type="radio" class="bool-@html\
11   Field" onchange="javascript:$('#@htmlField').val(\
12   false);" /> No
13       </label>
14
15       @if (ViewData.ModelMetadata.IsNullableVal\
16   ueType)
17       {
18           <label class="btn btn-info @noSelecti\
19   on">
20               <input type="radio" class="bool-@\
21   htmlField" onclick="javascript:$('#@htmlField').v\
22   al('');" />Do Not Set
23           </label>
24       }
25
26   </div>
```

There are two important pieces to note in the above code, namely the inspection of TemplateInfo and ModelMetadata in the ViewData instance presented to our view, and the hidden backing field that is kept in sync via JavaScript. ViewData is a ViewDataDictionary that contains, as those properties suggest, metadata about the type of model being used, information about the template, and other view-specific data.

To see this new template in action we'll have to get a Create view set up and an action on our controller. Head back to the `SimpleController` class and add the following code:

```
1  public ActionResult Create()
2  {
3      var person = new Person();
4      return View(person);
5  }
```

Now, right-click on the name of the method, and select "Add View...", then set it up to use the Create template for the `Person` class.

Creating a strongly-typed view

Visual Studio will throw you into the editor for your new view, and you can press CTRL+F5 to see your new default control for Boolean values, or navigate to http://localhost:*port*/Simple/Create to see the page.

The scaffolded view contains simple calls to HTML helpers and doesn't know anything about the instance of the Person that will be created or the fact that you've created a new template to render Boolean values. You'll only see the following:

```
1   @Html.EditorFor(model => model.LikesMusic)
```

As well, the templates are rendered on the fly by the view engine (just like all views) so you don't need to recompile as you make updates. Feel free to experiment with the template code and just refresh in your browser after you save.

Note that our Person class doesn't have a nullable Boolean value, but it if did, it would render like so because of our evaluation of the ModelMetadata in the template above:

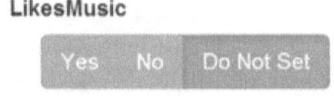

Nullable values rendered in our editor control

Controlling the Use of Custom Templates

Now these new controls – button groups for input and labels for display – work great, but you may not wish to use them for all Boolean properties. In both the DisplayTemplates and EditorTemplates folders, rename the Boolean template to BooleanButtonLabel.cshtml. Then, return to your Person class and decorate the LikesMusic property as follows:

```
1   [UIHint("BooleanButtonLabel")]
2   public bool LikesMusic { get; set; }
```

There may be scenarios where you wish to use several alternate templates to display or edit data. This attribute gives the MVC Framework directions to use a template of our choosing, rather than having to use the same template for all properties for the same type.

Chapter 8 Summary

While the default methods to render basic types are adequate, we often want to give our users an experience that is differnt than out-of-box. We have the freedom to do so in the MVC Framework by use of Display and Editor templates. In this chapter we built out the editor side of the equation, evaluating the model's metadata and other properties to correctly render a custom control for a specific type, namely, a group of styled radio buttons for Boolean values. We also implemented it such a way that we can control which properties the template is used for.

9. Templates for Complex Types

Sites like Facebook and Twitter or any site with a "feed" often present their data in a stream of "cards" or "blocks" that are repeatable and consistent, regardless of where you see the snippet of data. Let's take the UI we created for the Person, augment it a little bit and then make it reusable wherever we might want it displayed.

 Estimated time: Less than 10 minutes

Extracting the Person Template

We're going to build from the idea of using the DisplayTemplates in our ViewsShared folder, and add another file in there called Person.cshtml. Just right-click on the ViewsSharedDisplayTemplates folder and click Add –> View. Name the view Person, use the empty template and create it as a partial.

Now paste the following code into the file:

```
1   @model SimpleSite.Models.Person
2
3   <hr />
4   <div class="row">
5       <div class="col-md-2">
6           <img src="http://placehold.it/150x150" />
7       </div>
8       <div class="col-md-8">
9           <h3>@Model.FirstName @Model.LastName</h3>
10          <p>@Model.FirstName was born on @Model.Bi\
11  rthDate.ToString("D").</p>
12          <p>Likes Music: @Html.DisplayFor(model =>\
13  model.LikesMusic)</p>
14          @{
15              ViewBag.ListDescription = "Skills:";
16              Html.RenderPartial("_StringCollection\
17  ", Model.Skills);
18          }
19      </div>
20  </div>
```

An HR tag is dropped in there so that, down the road, should we display several Person objects sequentially we will have a nice divider. I've added the row class to a container DIV to keep elements of the template together and to reduce the risk of formatting running over or outside of the desired part of our doc.

Most of this you should recognize as fairly close to the code we were using in our Index view for the SimpleController. Above, I've added some columns and a placeholder image so that we can later give users an avatar. But I'm otherwise continuing to use the same elements we were building off of before, such as the DisplayFor and RenderPartial bits we've been working on.

Adding a simple placeholder image helps to figure out your layout and relay your suggested design to other stakeholders in your project. It is relatively painless to do with the free placehold.it[1] image service. You can control color, size and format, or even add your own text to the image.

Updating the Index View

The end result is that our Index view can be _much _simpler than it was. Here is what you need for the whole view source of Index.cshtml:

```
1   @model SimpleSite.Models.Person
2   @{
3       ViewBag.Title = "Index";
4   }
5
6   <div class="page-header">
7       <h1>Welcome to the Person Page <small>Read al\
8   l about @Model.FirstName</small></h1>
9   </div>
10
11  @Html.DisplayForModel(Model)
```

No longer do we have conditional class attributes nor any logic of any other kind. Our view is now just...doing view stuff. You'll find this extremely pleasant to work with in larger projects, where you're typically doing more than just putting a single entity on the page. With complex view models that contain many types or flattened types, display templates for complex types do a lot to help you keep your project easy to read and maintain.

_____

[1]http://placehold.it

Under the Covers

The `DisplayForModel` tries to find a display template that matches the type of model that is passed in, and sure enough, naming our partial view above "Person" and placing it in the Views\Shared\DisplayTemplates folder was all we needed to do to wire that up. It's another example of "convention over configuration" at work in the MVC Framework. Much of the same strategy is used to resolve the template by iterating over the partial views in our project that correspond to the type we're trying to style. You can have this happen implicitly through file naming as we have done here, or you can do it explicitly by using the appropriate attribute to decorate your class.

I've used only one set of layout classes as styles for my person template. In Chapter 15 we'll talk about Bootstrap's grid layout system, including how to make this even more reusable by introducing classes that allow the content to be rendered on different devices and screen sizes.

Chapter 9 Summary

A complex type is treated in much the same way as the basic Boolean type we created a template for in the previous chapter, allowing us to extract templates to increase usability as well as to simplify our views. In this chapter we did just that, extracting a display template for the `Person` class and cleaning up our view considerably.

10. HtmlHelper Extension Methods

As we extracted our Person template we stubbed in a placeholder for a person's avatar. Rather than creating our own system for uploading, resizing and storing the images, we'll use a commonly used service on the internet called Gravatar to display one that many users might already have.

 Estimated time: About 15 minutes

A Gravatar Extension Method

The format for Gravatar images is as follows:

http://www.gravatar.com/avatar/MD5HASH?options[1]

The MD5 hash is computed based on their email address, and there are a few options worth noting. Below are the querystring parameters we'll be using to generate our image.

- **Default Image**: the image or type of image to use or generate if there isn't a Gravatar for the specified email address.
- **Size**: the size of the image to be returned, always a square.

---

[1]http://www.gravatar.com/avatar/MD5HASH?options

- **Rating**: users self-specify their rating and can use different
  avatars for different audiences.

We'll represent those options in an class that we'll use as a parameter. Create a Helpers folder, then create a class called GravatarOptions
in it. We're going to use this class to serve defaults and help make
it easier to create Gravatar images from our page when we want
something outside of the norm.

```
1  public class GravatarOptions
2  {
3      public string DefaultImageType { get; set; }
4      public string RatingLevel { get; set; }
5      public int Size { get; set; }
6
7      public class DefaultImage
8      {
9          public const string Default = "";
10         public const string Http404 = "404";
11         public const string MysteryMan = "mm";
12         public const string Identicon = "identico\
13 n";
14         public const string MonsterId = "monsteri\
15 d";
16         public const string Wavatar = "wavatar";
17         public const string Retro = "retro";
18     }
19
20     public class Rating
21     {
22         public const string G = "g";
23         public const string PG = "pg";
24         public const string R = "r";
25         public const string X = "x";
```

```
26        }
27
28
29        internal static GravatarOptions GetDefaults()
30        {
31            return new GravatarOptions
32            {
33                DefaultImageType = GravatarOptions.De\
34 faultImage.Retro,
35                Size = 150,
36                RatingLevel = GravatarOptions.Rating.G
37            };
38        }
39 }
```

And finally, add a class called GravatarHelper, then add the code below:

```
1  public static class GravatarHelper
2  {
3      public static HtmlString GravatarImage(this H\
4  tmlHelper htmlHelper, string emailAddress, Gravat\
5  arOptions options = null)
6      {
7          if (options == null)
8              options = GravatarOptions.GetDefaults\
9  ();
10
11         var imgTag = new TagBuilder("img");
12
13         emailAddress = string.IsNullOrEmpty(email\
14 Address) ? string.Fmpty : emailAddress.Trim().Tol\
15 ower();
16
```

```
17          imgTag.Attributes.Add("src",
18              string.Format("http://www.gravatar.co\
19  m/avatar/{0}?s={1}{2}{3}",
20              GetMd5Hash(emailAddress),
21              options.Size,
22              "&d=" + options.DefaultImageType,
23              "&r=" + options.RatingLevel
24              )
25          );
26
27          return new HtmlString(imgTag.ToString(Tag\
28  RenderMode.SelfClosing));
29      }
30
31      // Source: http://msdn.microsoft.com/en-us/li\
32  brary/system.security.cryptography.md5.aspx
33      private static string GetMd5Hash(string input)
34      {
35          byte[] data = MD5.Create().ComputeHash(En\
36  coding.UTF8.GetBytes(input));
37          var sBuilder = new StringBuilder();
38          for (int i = 0; i < data.Length; i++)
39          {
40              sBuilder.Append(data[i].ToString("x2"\
41  ));
42          }
43          return sBuilder.ToString();
44      }
45  }
```

There are two methods in here, the extension method that generates the HtmlString containing the element we need to render the Gravatar, and a crypto method that helps us generate the hash we need to supply to Gravatar when we request the image.

Extension methods accept the type you are extending as the first parameter and operate on the instance of the object, though they are defined as a static. This may help understand why you must pass the first parameter as the type you want to extend with the *this* modifier. You can then optionally add any additional parameters that you will need to work with. For us, we're just accepting the email address and a GravatarOptions instance.

In our helper, we create a tag builder for images, then build the URL based on the options the user has provided following the requirements that the image hosting provider has spelled out. If our callers haven't provided the options parameter, we simply load a set of defaults from our options class above.

 This is an overly-simplified version of Andrew Free-mantle's[2] work on his Gravatar-HtmlHelper[3] project on GitHub. Please visit his project for a more complete implementation.

Using the Gravatar in our Person Template

Our HTML helper will work like any other HTML helper, but we need to let the MVC Framework know where to find it. To do so, we'll have to go and add the namespace to our Web.Config in our Views folder (located at Views\Web.Config). We could also add a using statement to each page where we want to use our helper, but adding it to the web config file makes it globally available throughout our views. Add the following to the Razor namespaces section in that file:

---

[2]https://github.com/AndrewFreemantle
[3]https://github.com/AndrewFreemantle/Gravatar-HtmlHelper

```
1  <add namespace="SimpleSite.Helpers"/>
```

We'll need an email address, so add the following property in Person.cs.

```
1  public string EmailAddress { get; set; }
```

Next, jump back into your SimpleController class and update the instantiation of the person object so that they have a value in there:

```
1  var person = new Person
2  {
3      FirstName = "Billy Jo",
4      LastName = "McGuffery",
5      BirthDate = new DateTime(1990, 6,1),
6      LikesMusic = true,
7      EmailAddress = "Bill@jo.com",
8      Skills = new List<string>() { "Math", "Scienc\
9  e", "History" }
10 };
```

Now, update your Person.cshtml template by replacing the IMG tag with the following:

```
1  @Html.GravatarImage(Model.EmailAddress)
```

Then, pop into your browser to see the fruits of your effort!

Welcome to the Person Page Read all about Billy Jo

Billy Jo McGuffery

Billy Jo was born on Friday, June 1, 1990.

Likes Music: Yes

Skills: Math Science History

A Person Profile with a Gravatar

The Gravatar image will be updated for any email address that you put in. You can try playing with the different defaults, your own email address or other options.

> I wouldn't actually advocate creating you own, full implementation of an `HtmlHelper` method for Gravatars. The point of this exercise was to walk through a simple implementation, but there are much more complete helpers available on NuGet. These are open source, ready to be deployed to your app, and likely looking for someone to help keep the code maintained.

Chapter 10 Summary

We've been making efforts along the way to simplify our views whenever the opportunity presents itself. When it comes to doing something like generating a hash of an email address, this is definitely something we don't want to be doing in our view, even if we can. This chapter gave an overview of extension methods and provided a simple, but relevant implementation that we can use in our project to display a user's avatar.

11. Realistic Test Data for Our View

If a controller deals with a certain type of data – say, entities of the Person type – the index will typically contain a collection of data of that type, or perhaps some other related interface (such as search or filter capabilities, or partial views of related data). Let's add a PersonController and get a feel for what that looks like.

 Estimated time: About 15 minutes

Creating the Person Controller

Back in Chapter 3 we added a SimpleController to our project. Use the same approach to create a new, empty controller now called PersonController in the same folder of your solution. The Index method is the only one in the class, but it's going to need some data.

 There are a number of controller templates available that can be used to quickly generate different levels of CRUD capabilities using a variety of data access strategies. While you may find these useful in certain scenarios you will find in the long run that they usually only serve the basic cases. You'll see another sample of this scaffolding in Chapter 25 that can either be used in a Minimal Viable Product demonstration or as a base to create something more elaborate.

Generating Realistic Test Data

Now, we have a couple of options to get data:

- We can hand-bomb 25 (or 5 or 10 or 100) entries into some kind of text file taking however much time our manager allows or requires
- We can new up dozens of objects with copy & paste and have 60 of the exact same person.
- Or, we can take a less self-deprecating approach and use a test data generator while we flush out our application and get realistic test data with minimum effort. Let's try that!

AngelaSmith is an open source library that contains internal databases of text and several strategies to try to create objects for you, filling in the properties with realistic data. Fields that look like they should contain a phone number get a phone number, a property called EmailAddress will get an email address. Being a DLL, it's easy to add to any existing project. Being a NuGet package makes it even easier to do so.

Go to your Package Manager Console. If you don't see that window, it's typically located in the bottom of Visual Studio in one of the tabs. If you still don't see it, try opening it from View -> Other Windows -> Package Manager Console.

Now, let's install a package that will generate our data for us, the previously discussed AngelaSmith. Type the following command in the Package Manager Console:

```
1  Install-Package AngelaSmith -Version 1.0.1
```

You should see confirmation that the package is installed.

Note that at the time of this writing you will be required to use the very specific version 1.0.1 of AngelaSmith to ensure the data is correctly generated inside an MVC application. This is due to some recent enhancements that didn't turn out to be too enhancing after all. At some point down the road, this will be corrected and you will be able to use the more advanced features of the newer versions of the library.

Configuring AngelaSmith

We'll need a place to store the data that is generated, so at the class level, add a static field.

```
1   private static ICollection<Person> _people;
```

We're making it static so that we don't have to recreate the data on each page load, just when the app starts up. Now add a static controller to configure the data generator.

```
1   static PersonController()
2   {
3       _people = Angie.Configure<Person>()
4           .Fill(p => p.BirthDate)
5           .AsPastDate()
6           .Fill(p => p.LikesMusic)
7           .WithRandom(new List<bool>(){true, true, \
8   true, false, false})
9           .Fill(p => p.Skills, () => new List<strin\
10  g>() { "Math", "Science", "History" })
11          .MakeList<Person>(20);
12  }
```

It might seem like a lot is going on, but it's actually quite straightforward. First is a call to the Configure method to enter configuration mode.

```
1   _people = Angie.Configure<Person>()
```

Then we have three `Fill` statements that demonstrate a few of the ways that we can generate data. For example, you can get a date from the past, fill a property with a random value (60% of the time `LikesMusic` will be true), or, here, use a lambda to set up an anonymous function to populate the value.

```
1   .Fill(p => p.Skills, () => new List<string>() { "\
2   Math", "Science", "History" })
```

Finally, we call the `MakeList` method to get the list of 20 entities. By default, it will generate 25 but you can specify however many you like.

```
1   .MakeList<Person>(20);
```

Adding the Index View

We'll need to pass the view some data, when it's ready, so let's now update our `Index` method so that it does that.

```
1   public ActionResult Index()
2   {
3       return View(_people);
4   }
```

You're going to like this part. Add an empty View to the project by right-clicking on the Index method of the `PersonController`. Then add the following code:

```
1  @model IEnumerable<SimpleSite.Models.Person>
2
3  @Html.DisplayForModel(Model)
```

Yeup! That's it! Run your site to see your list of peeps!

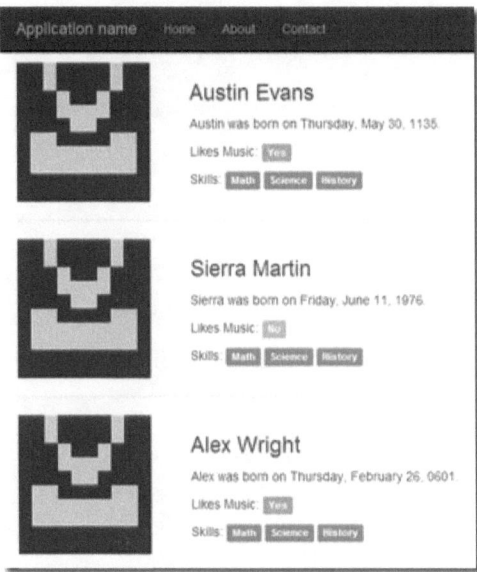

Magnificent! Data We Didn't Have to Create!

Chapter 11 Summary

It's great when things really start to come together, when we finally get to start to play with the Lego pieces we've been creating along the way. In this chapter we basically removed a lot of code, and wrote two new lines relevant to our project, but we have a list of Person entities displaying with nearly no effort. HtmlHelpers, partial views and display templates coming together to make light lifting for great results.

We also had a chance to use the AngelaSmith library which, like the placehold.it image service gives us a way to stub out our interface before we get real data.

III Exploring Bootstrap

12. Implement Search Using Inline Forms and AJAX

It had to happen; at some point we were going to need to let our users enter some data! Well, that time has come, so let's start by adding a handy-dandy search form to our Person page.

HTML forms will typically need a few cues on how to properly render themselves and take part in Booststrap's style party of awesome. Let's get a search form going and start filtering our results.

 Estimated time: About 20 minutes

Adding the Search Bar

There are actually a few styles of forms that you can get going. A standard styling gives you label-over-control type layout, horizontal forms give you label-beside-control layout and inline styling gives you controls without labels side-by-each continuously in the row. That's the one we'll go with to generate our simple search form:

Providing Search UI

Create a partial view under the Views\Person folder. You can make it an empty one, and call it _PersonSearchForm.cshtml. Paste in the following code:

```
1   <hr/>
2   <div class="container">
3       <div class="pull-right">
4           <form class="form-inline" role="form">
5               <div class="form-group">
6                   <label class="sr-only" for="searc\
7   h-text">Email address</label>
8                   <input type="text" class="form-co\
9   ntrol" id="search-text" placeholder="Enter Search\
10  Text">
11                  </div>
12                  <button type="button" class="btn btn-\
13  success" id="search-btn">Search</button>
14              </form>
15          </div>
16  </div>
```

We have a few things going on here:

- The HR tag is just a style thing and not required. It makes the search form look more "balanced" vertically on the form.
- There is a DIV that acts as a container, keeping our content separate from the rest of the page. It is a wrapper for a "pull-right" styled DIV that moves our search bar over to the right hand side of the page.
- The form is given a class of "form-inline". This is the first important part of making our controls and labels show up correctly.
- Inside that FORM element we have a DIV with a class of "form-group". This lets Bootstrap know (or rather, the browser through Bootstrap's CSS) that these controls are related in some way. Specifically, we have a label for an input.
- Because this is an "inline" form, we're using the "sr-only" class on the label to eat the display and keep the visuals tidy.

"SR" stands for "Screen Reader"; this is an accessibility tag.

When the form data comes calling, we're going to need someone to answer the phone on the controller side.

The Controller's Search Method

In your PersonController class, add the following public method:

```
 1  public ActionResult SearchPeople(string searchTex\
 2  t)
 3  {
 4      var term = searchText.ToLower();
 5      var result = _people
 6          .Where(p =>
 7              p.FirstName.ToLower().Contains(term) \
 8  ||
 9              p.LastName.ToLower().Contains(term)
10          );
11
12      return PartialView("_SearchPeople", result);
13  }
```

This accepts a string parameter and finds any matches where FirstName or LastName match what the user entered, then it returns via a call to PartialView to generate the result. We're using a partial because we don't want to have to reload the entire page each time the user clicks the search button.

> A quick note: the astute reader will note that that this simplified method of search won't pass the Turkey Test[1]. If you work with different cultures, this is a great

---

[1]http://www.moserware.com/2008/02/does-your-code-pass-turkey-test.html

side-read, and you'll need to approach the problem in a different way.

When we call `PartialView` the MVC Framework doesn't attempt to resolve or render a full layout, so we just get the meat that lives in the cshtml file itself and as processed by the view engine. Rendered via the controller, we have to pass in our data as a parameter. If you were rendering a partial via a View (with an `HtmlHelper`) the partial could 'inherit' the parent page's model and use that to render your content. The partial we need should be located in Views\Person\ and called _SearchPeople.cshtml and the code looks like the following:

```
1   @model IEnumerable<SimpleSite.Models.Person>
2
3   @Html.DisplayForModel(Model)
4
5   @if (!Model.Any())
6   {
7       <h3>Sorry!</h3>
8       <p>Looks like there's no results for that per\
9   son.</p>
10  }
```

Partial in place, controller set up to search...off to the core view.

Updating the View

Back in Views\Person\Index.cshtml there isn't a lot we have to do to get our form to display. Update the code so it reads as follows:

```
1  @model IEnumerable<SimpleSite.Models.Person>
2
3  @{ Html.RenderPartial("_PersonSearchForm"); }
4
5  <div id="people-data">
6      @Html.DisplayForModel(Model)
7  </div>
```

I have updated the view from yesterday by wrapping the data with a DIV that acts as a container. We'll use that later when we AJAX up the page. Press CTRL+F5 to see the updated view in action.

Displaying the New Search Feature

This handles the display aspect, but we need some script in place to handle the button click and make the AJAX call, finally updating the page with the search results. Add a script section to the bottom of the page as follows:

```
1   @section scripts
2   {
3       <script type="text/javascript">
4           $(function () {
5               // it's lonely here...
6           });
7       </script>
8   }
```

> **Today's Bonus Content**: Sections are defined in the layout page that is used by your view. You can find them in Views\Shared_Layout.cshtml. These sections can be required or optional per your needs. The default template defines only the scripts section, but you may often wish to include something in the page header or footer.

Now the script doesn't do anything quite yet, except give us a place to land. What you see above is called a "self-executing anonymous method", which is a good term to know if you want to sound smart around your boss. Basically, jQuery will make sure any code in this block is executed in a cross-browser friendly way *after* the page is finished loading.

Replace that lonely comment with the following code:

```
1  $("#search-btn").click(function () {
2
3      var searchTerm = $("#search-text").val();
4
5      $.get("SearchPeople", { searchText: searchTer\
6  m })
7          .success(function(data) {
8              $("#people-data").html(data);
9          });
10
11 });
```

If you're not familiar with JavaScript or the patterns that jQuery uses, here's little breakdown of what is happening:

- A click event handler is setup for the element in the DOM that has an ID of "search-btn".
- The event handler is an anonymous method that invokes the jQuery get() method, passing in the action that we're targeting and the data that we're trying to pass in.
- The data we're passing in is read from the form and assigned to the searchText key
- When you pass in parameters from calls like this, you need to make sure spelling and case are identical to avoid rapid hair loss. Oh, and null values.
- The get() method follows the "promise" pattern, and you get to register a callback when the search is completed. Here, we use the success callback and pass it an anonymous method to be called for successful execution paths.
- Our anonymous callback method is invoked when the AJAX completes successfully and it updates the data container ("people-data") with the HTML that is returned from our controller.

Try typing in some search terms from your Person\Index page.

Bazinga! We have ourselves some search!

Chapter 12 Summary

The development of a great UI can quickly span multiple components working in concert to pull together the desired experience for the user. In this chapter we modified our controller, added an action, created an HTML form, recycled a partial view and added JavaScript to make an AJAX call.

13. Standard Styling and Horizontal Forms

We had a quick look at the inline styling for a search form in Chapter 12 giving us a way to build out search bars and other kinds of "single line" interfaces. While these are great for things like search, filtering or perhaps in-line edits, they don't settle the matter of general data input, and users are going to want to enter data.

In this chapter we'll have a closer look at the other types of styling, but first we'll make a quick pit stop to update our Person class so that we can take advantage of a few of the validation features of both MVC and the Bootstrap library.

 Estimated time: Less than 20 minutes

Updating our Person

Return to the model class for Person in the Models folder. We're going to need to do two things here, add a constructor (so we don't run into problems with null for the date and our collection) and make all fields except PersonId and Skills required. The Person class should look like this when you're done:

```
1   public class Person
2   {
3       public Person()
4       {
5           Skills = new HashSet<string>();
6           BirthDate = DateTime.Now.AddYears(-20);
7       }
8
9       public int PersonId { get; set; }
10
11      [Required]
12      public string FirstName { get; set; }
13
14      [Required]
15      public string LastName { get; set; }
16
17      [Required]
18      public DateTime BirthDate { get; set; }
19
20      [Required]
21      [UIHint("BooleanButtonLabel")]
22      public bool LikesMusic { get; set; }
23
24      [Required]
25      [EmailAddress]
26      public string EmailAddress { get; set; }
27
28      public ICollection<string> Skills { get; set;\
29  }
30  }
```

Note that on the EmailAddress, we also added an attribute called, well, EmailAddress. This is a pre-defined validation attribute that the MVC Framework uses to give us useful information in our controller, as well as to leverage client-side scripts for validation (to save round-tripping). Best of both worlds!

Allowing Create on Our Controller

Now we can pop into our controller and set things up for the create action. We'll need two methods – one for the GET and one for the POST. The GET method creates a default Person object and passes it to the view.

```
1   public ActionResult Create()
2   {
3       var person = new Person();
4       return View(person);
5   }
```

The POST method is decorated with an attribute and accepts an instance of Person back as a parameter. This is one of the really great features of the MVC Framework: while you still have access to the form collection and full request object, you don't have to deal with the cruft unless you want or need to; the Framework performs "model binding" for you and fills in the properties of the parameter objects you are expecting based on the names of the fields passed in.

```
1   [HttpPost]
2   public ActionResult Create(Person person)
3   {
4       if (ModelState.IsValid)
5       {
6           _people.Add(person);
7           return RedirectToAction("Index");
8       }
9
10      return View(person);
11  }
```

The base Controller class that we inherit from also gives us some rich capabilities for evaluating the incoming parameter. We can inspect some simple pre-checked values, add validation error messages and deal with the user input as we see fit.

We are able to check ModelState.IsValid because we setup our model to require certain fields. You can add all kinds of validations to cover min and max values, ranges, matches based on Regexes, or, as we did, a check to make sure an email address is valid. There are more still, and you can create your own if you like for both client- and server-side validation.

Generating the View

Now, you've done the exercise of creating a view before but we're going to approach it a little differently here. This time, when you right-click on the Create method in the controller, be sure to select the correct template and options.

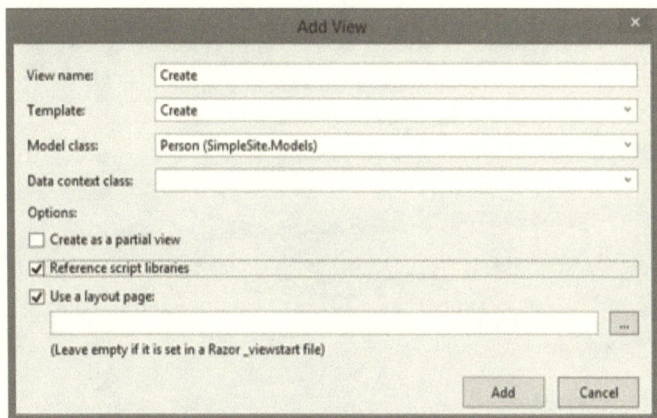

Scaffolding a Strongly-Typed Create View

It's a Create template, with the `Person` class as the model. You'll want to clear the partial checkbox if it's selected and make sure you "Include Script Libraries". Remember that leaving the name of the view as Create allows the framework to pick it up on it's own.

This One's Not Quite Free

The default view actually looks pretty good, in fact, you'd have to remove the form-horizontal style from the class attribute of the div (in the root of the form that is generated) to get the "standard" look-and-feel, which would be like this:

Create

Person

FirstName

LastName

BirthDate

6/13/1994 10:11:19 PM

LikesMusic

Yes   No

EmailAddress

Create

Back to List

A Form Lacking Some Style

But you'll notice that we're missing something in particular: a way to add skills to our person. Also, it looks way better with that form-horizontal class in there!

Getting Things Straight

So, if you removed that form-horizontal class, add it back. Then we're going to add the next little bit of markup, right before the submit button on the form:

```
<div class="form-group">
    @Html.LabelFor(model => model.Skills, htmlAtt\
ributes: new { @class = "control-label col-md-2" \
})
    <div class="col-md-10">
        <div class="input-group">
            <span class="input-group-btn">
                <button class="btn btn-default" i\
d="add-skill" type="button">
                    <span class="glyphicon glyphi\
```

```
11  con-plus"></span>
12                  </button>
13              </span>
14              <input type="text" id="skill" class="\
15  form-control" placeholder="Type, then click + to \
16  add" />
17          </div>
18      </div>
19  </div>
20
21  <div id="skills-wrapper"></div>
22
23  <div class="form-group">
24      <div class="col-md-offset-2 col-md-10">
25          <ul id="skills-list" class="list-group"><\
26  /ul>
27      </div>
28  </div>
```

You'll notice that we don't actually have any new form elements here that will submit with the form (the input there doesn't have a name and won't appear in the submitted form collection), but we have a textbox that lets you enter some text.

A Simple Way to Append to a List

There is an empty DIV there that we'll use to add hidden text inputs to the form via jQuery. We also have a styled UL list in there that we'll use to display what has already been added.

We'll add the following script to make that markup tick, which you can add at the bottom of the scaffolded script section in Create.cshtml:

```
1  <script>
2     $(function () {
3        $("#add-skill").click(function () {
4           // get the value of the added skill
5           var skill = $("#skill").val();
6
7           // push hidden input to our form
8           $("#skills-wrapper").append($("<input\
9  type='hidden' name='Skills' value='" + skill + "\
10 ' />"));
11
12          // add list item for display purposes
13          $("#skills-list").append($("<li class\
14 ='list-group-item'>" + skill + "</li>"));
15
16          // reset the form
17          $("#skill").val("").focus();
18       });
19    });
20 </script>
```

The comments in the script lay out the goal here, essentially that we're going to grab the value from the entry box and turn it into both a hidden form element and an LI in that unordered list we created earlier. Finally, we reset the input and set the focus.

Here it is in action!

Skills	✚	Type, then click + to add

Music Appreciation

Singing Along to Disney Tunes

Counting Stars

List Items Added to the Form

I Really Like This Part

Remember how we didn't add any form elements with the name "Skills"? Well, we did in our JavaScript. In fact, we'll add as many *hidden* form elements with the same name, "Skills", to the form as the user would like. What happens to those form elements with the same name?

In your controller, in the POST method you added, set a breakpoint *anywhere* in the code, then navigate to your Create page and fill out the form. When you submit, you'll be able to inspect the Skills property of the person...the MVC Framework model binding is smart enough to see multiple instances of the same-named form element (in our case, a hidden text element) that has the name of a property in our model.

You can verify that the payload coming from the client contained several of those form elements by inspecting the request when you hit your breakpoint. Model binding kicks in, news up a collection for us, populates it with the values and puts it into our Person parameter. Sweet!

Chapter 13 Summary

Validation is an important part of every web application, and both Bootstrap and the MVC Framework have ways of helping us determine model validity and to relay that information to our user. Here, we added attributes to our model to instruct the MVC Framework on how to evaluate those properties. We used the built-in capabilities provided through the base controller to check those properties before saving to the database. And, on the client side of things, we constructed a UI that gave the user the ability to submit a list of items to the server in a way that takes advantage of the model binding capabilities of MVC.

14. Bootstrap Alerts and MVC Framework TempData

Something may go wrong, or it may go right. It may go smooth or go bump in the night. And, at various times, your application will want to let the user know about it. **Bootstrap** has a component called an Alert that works quite nicely for these types of information.

Oh snap! Change a few things up and try submitting again.

Aww, sad face. That's not what we wanted!

Likewise, the **MVC Framework** has a great place where we can store these messages without having to worry about postbacks, short term storage or the like. Pairing these two features up makes a great way to relay information to the user.

 Estimated time: About 20 minutes

A Few More Helpers

We'll try to take a bit of a structured approach to put our alerts in place, and we'll do that by using some basic types to compose our messages and help format them. Add another class file to your project in the Helpers namespace (located in the \Helpers folder), and drop in the following code:

```
1   public class Alert
2   {
3       public const string TempDataKey = "TempDataAl\
4   erts";
5
6       public string AlertStyle { get; set; }
7       public string Message { get; set; }
8       public bool Dismissable { get; set; }
9   }
10
11  public static class AlertStyles
12  {
13      public const string Success = "success";
14      public const string Information = "info";
15      public const string Warning = "warning";
16      public const string Danger = "danger";
17  }
```

These classes give us some constants to help render our Bootstrap alerts, as well as a class to help store and pass data around.

Base Controller - *Almost* A Best Practice

One of the first things you will likely do on any MVC project is to start with a new base controller that you will inherit from instead of the built-in Controller that ships with the framework.

While that may seem like a weird suggestion coming from a guy who likes the YAGNI principle, I've never worked on a project that didn't have a base controller, end up with one, or at least couldn't have used one. There will be valid cases where you won't need one, and likely several cases where multiple base controllers will be required, so it's debatable as to whether or not it should be a rule.

This part is a best practice, however: don't let your base classes get "fat", loaded with code you're not using 90% of the time.

At any rate, if you choose to use base classes or not, for this project we will and ours will look like this:

```
1  public class BaseController : Controller
2  {
3      public void Success(string message, bool dism\
4  issable = false)
5      {
6          AddAlert(AlertStyles.Success, message, di\
7  smissable);
8      }
9
10     public void Information(string message, bool \
11 dismissable = false)
12     {
13         AddAlert(AlertStyles.Information, message\
14 , dismissable);
15     }
16
17     public void Warning(string message, bool dism\
18 issable = false)
19     {
20         AddAlert(AlertStyles.Warning, message, di\
21 smissable);
22     }
23
24     public void Danger(string message, bool dismi\
25 ssable = false)
26     {
27         AddAlert(AlertStyles.Danger, message, dis\
28 missable);
```

```
29        }
30
31      private void AddAlert(string alertStyle, stri\
32  ng message, bool dismissable)
33      {
34          var alerts = TempData.ContainsKey(Alert.T\
35  empDataKey)
36              ? (List<Alert>)TempData[Alert.TempDat\
37  aKey]
38              : new List<Alert>();
39
40          alerts.Add(new Alert
41          {
42              AlertStyle = alertStyle,
43              Message = message,
44              Dismissable = dismissable
45          });
46
47          TempData[Alert.TempDataKey] = alerts;
48      }
49
50  }
```

These methods are going to help us record and render alerts from our controller and into our views. There are four pretty similar calls going on there that keep the helper strings away from our controllers. The AddAlert method takes care of fetching or creating a list of alerts.

We're using TempData here for storage which is good for the next *completed* request from the server to the same client. That could be the current request, should we complete execution and render a view, or that could be the immediately *next* request, should we decide to redirect the user.

Using a list of Alerts gives us the ability to add more than one type of alert, or several instances of alerts to the page at once. If you consider things like ActionFilters (don't worry, those are coming) that have an opportunity to interact with the execution pipeline, you won't ever know exactly what parts of your application might be trying to signal something to the user.

Note: I got the idea for this approach through working with Eric Hexter[1] on the Twitter.Bootstrap.Mvc[2] project before Bootstrap was included by default. In that version, Eric's implementation allowed for one message per alert type, but it was definitely what got the ball rolling for me on this one.

Updates to PersonController

Start by changing the declaration to inherit from our spanky new base class.

```
1  public class PersonController : BaseController
```

Then, update your create method to use the new methods we've added.

---

[1]https://twitter.com/ehexter
[2]https://github.com/erichexter/twitter.bootstrap.mvc

```
1   [HttpPost]
2   public ActionResult Create(Person person)
3   {
4       if (ModelState.IsValid)
5       {
6           _people.Add(person);
7           Success(string.Format("<b>{0}</b> was suc\
8   cessfully added to the database.", person.FirstNa\
9   me), true);
10          return RedirectToAction("Index");
11      }
12      Danger("Looks like something went wrong. Plea\
13  se check your form.");
14      return View(person);
15  }
```

We've made it super easy to store various alerts which will hang around in memory until we complete a request. In the case of the happy path above, the Success message hangs around on the server until the client requests the redirected content. For the Danger message on the sad path, the view is immediately returned and the TempData is cleared.

Showing our Alerts

While we could just put all the info we need into the layout, we can keep our code cleaner by using a partial view to render the alerts. Under Views\Shared, add a new partial view called _Alerts.cshtml and put in the following code:

```
1   @using SimpleSite.Models
2   @{
3       var alerts = TempData.ContainsKey(Alert.TempD\
4   ataKey)
5                   ? (List<Alert>)TempData[Alert.Tem\
6   pDataKey]
7                   : new List<Alert>();
8
9       if (alerts.Any())
10      {
11          <hr/>
12      }
13
14      foreach (var alert in alerts)
15      {
16          var dismissableClass = alert.Dismissable \
17  ? "alert-dismissable" : null;
18          <div class="alert alert-@alert.AlertStyle\
19   @dismissableClass">
20              @if (alert.Dismissable)
21              {
22                  <button type="button" class="clos\
23  e" data-dismiss="alert" aria-hidden="true">&times\
24  ;</button>
25              }
26              @Html.Raw(alert.Message)
27          </div>
28      }
29  }
```

We grab the alerts out of the TempData (if they exist) and then loop through each one, rendering them in the order they were added. If they had the Dismissable flag set to true, we also render the appropriate Bootstrap elements and styles to make the alert go away on command.

Now update your _Layout.cshtml to include the call to render the partial view. Your container with the call to RenderBody() should now look like this:

```
<div class="container body-content">
    @{ Html.RenderPartial("_Alerts"); }
    @RenderBody()
    <hr />
    <footer>
        <p>&copy; @DateTime.Now.Year - My ASP.NET\
Application</p>
    </footer>
</div>
```

And now, after you add a new person to the list, you'll see a nicely formatted, dismissable alert at the top of the page.

James was successfully added to the database.   ✕

An alert rendered to the page

Chapter 14 Summary

We've been shuffling around a bit between concepts to get thinking and form a few ideas about how the Asp.Net MVC Framework and Bootstrap can work together. In this chapter we took the alert styling available through Bootstrap and made it possible to render it from anywhere in our application that has a tie to our new BaseController. We again maintained our focus on keeping our UI clean, and pushed the markup required for alerts out to its own partial view, meaning we only needed one line of code in our layout.

15. Some Bootstrap Basics

Through the chapters so far we've started to see what Bootstrap can do, but how does it get there? Why does the default page look like it does? And what are some of these classes we've been using?

 Estimated time: Less than 15 minutes

The Shell That Makes it Tick

Bootstrap is a responsive grid style and JavaScript library that makes some assumptions about the kind of project you'll be creating:

- You care about mobile users
- You want a familiar UX for your users
- You are targeting clients capable of HTML5, CSS and JavaScript
- You like the look and feel of Bootstrap, or you: a) know how to change it, or, b) you have a theme you want to use.

People, there are no more excuses for using tables for layout! Unless, of course, you have a table of data you want to display. You can use the CSS of Bootstrap on it's own and make use of the built in styles to control the layout of your pages, accommodating for different screen sizes and device resolutions.

JavaScript isn't a requirement for your site, but anything beyond the basic CSS will need to support it. In some cases, functionality of simple controls is augmented or simply made possible by virtue of the JavaScript library. What does Bootstrap's JavaScript have to offer?

- It provides a programmatic API for components and elements of the page
- It establishes custom events for actions unique to the Bootstrap controls
- It gives the ability to automatically wire up components on your page – almost akin to "programming" it on the page, but using Data Attributes in your markup.
- It provides a no-conflict mode to operate with other client-side frameworks
- It allows components with heavier processing costs to be delay-initiated, making your page look and feel faster

One Grid to...Line Up Them All

Imagine dividing your page up into 12 columns, and using a row to hold those columns, and putting all your rows into a container. Then, you choose if you want to assume a series of "responsive" widths, or a fluid width that is calculated on the fly to control the size of your columns. In a nutshell, that is what a grid layout system is doing for you.

Check out these samples from the template. Your home page looks like this in a desktop browser on a larger screen resolution:

But when you scale it down, you get the following without having to completely design an alternate site:

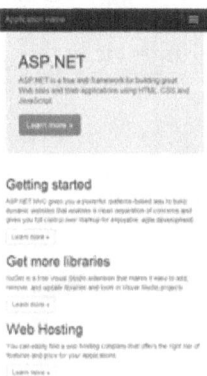

The Default Template on a Narrow (Mobile) Screen

The grid capabilities give you many options for how you want to tackle your layout regardless of the user's viewport. **This is significant because you don't have to write your site twice**. There was previous emphasis on making a "mobile friendly version" of your site, but the Bootstrap opinion on design is that you should be mobile first. If you're choosing to build a new site on some greenfield project it is worth spending some time on how the grid breaks down.

The best way to do this is to visit the Grid Template[1] sample site to see how the different arrangements of classes work together.

The MVC Framework's Home Page

Consider those images above from your project's home page, and have a look at what's going on. There is a menu at the top of the page that automatically collapses into a mobile-friendly arrangement when the screen size gets smaller.

---

[1]http://getbootstrap.com/examples/grid/

The Collapsed Menu

The code for this navbar control is in the _Layout.cshtml file.

```
1  <div class="navbar navbar-inverse navbar-fixed-to\
2  p">
3      <div class="container">
4          <div class="navbar-header">
5              <button type="button" class="navbar-t\
6  oggle" data-toggle="collapse" data-target=".navba\
7  r-collapse">
8                  <span class="icon-bar"></span>
9                  <span class="icon-bar"></span>
10                 <span class="icon-bar"></span>
11             </button>
12             @Html.ActionLink("Application name", \
13  "Index", "Home", new { area = "" }, new { @class \
14  = "navbar-brand" })
15         </div>
16         <div class="navbar-collapse collapse">
17             <ul class="nav navbar-nav">
18                 <li>@Html.ActionLink("Home", "Ind\
19  ex", "Home")</li>
20                 <li>@Html.ActionLink("About", "Ab\
21  out", "Home")</li>
22                 <li>@Html.ActionLink("Contact", "\
23  Contact", "Home")</li>
24             </ul>
25             @Html.Partial("_LoginPartial")
26         </div>
27     </div>
28  </div>
```

There are two DIVs inside the inner container, one the header, the second a collapsable section that is displayed on the same row. On smaller screens, that section disappears in favor of the button in the header. The wiring for all this is done with data attributes.

The links in the header are either rendered in that row, or in a mobile-friendly stack of links when the navbar is collapsed.

See those three spans in there? Those use a class called icon-bar from the Bootstrap library that looks like this:

```
1  .navbar-toggle .icon-bar {
2    display: block;
3    width: 22px;
4    height: 2px;
5    border-radius: 1px;
6  }
```

While I'm assuming they could have used an image or something from Glyphicon here, this is a very light-weight way to render the now familiar "hey I got more stuff for you to look at" iconography that many mobile users are accustomed to.

The rest of the content on the page is rendered in Index.cshtml inside the Views\Home folder.

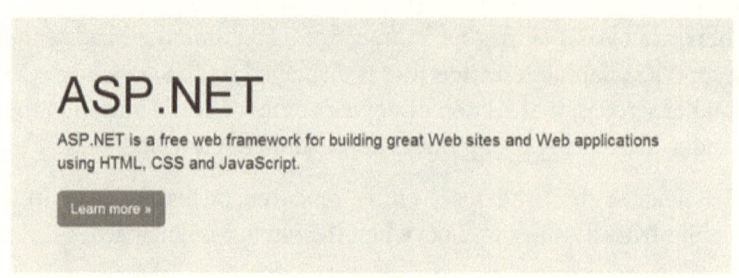

The 'Main' Content of the Home Page

There are two parts in play here, a jumbotron component and a row with three equally-sized columns. The jumbotron is the grey area with the larger title. It assumes the full width of the container it resides in, and gives a few extra style classes to help make content stand out.

```
1  <div class="jumbotron">
2      <h1>ASP.NET</h1>
3      <p class="lead">ASP.NET is a free...</p>
4      <p><a href="http://asp.net" class="btn btn-pr\
5  imary btn-lg">Learn more &raquo;</a></p>
6  </div>
```

The three bits of content are basically assembles as follows:

```
1   <div class="row">
2       <!-- Three of these -->
3       <div class="col-md-4">
4           <h2>Getting started</h2>
5           <p>Content...</p>
6           <p><a class="btn btn-default" href="http:\
7   //...">Learn more &raquo;</a></p>
8       </div>
9   </div>
```

There are three DIV elements that have the col-md-4 (read: content targeting a minimum of a medium screen resolution and spanning 4 columns). These are all contained in the row DIV, and if they add up to 12 or less (3x4 = 12) then they are almost certain to end up on the same row.

Put on Your Explorer Hat

Be sure to punch around with the grid mechanics a little and check out the Views\Home\Index.cshtml source in full (above are just the snippets) to get a good grip on how the layout works. Or, try switching the container class on the _Layout to use container-fluid instead.

Understanding how the grid layout works, floats, collapses and resizes rows and columns will be a critical part of your design work.

Chapter 15 Summary

This chapter is really about understanding how the Bootstrap library comes together with JavaScript and CSS to help your design shine on any device, even if you're not a designer. Bootstrap provides consistent fonts, spacing and margins as well as a way to cleverly respond to different screen sizes.

16. Conceptual Organization of the Bootstrap Library

There are three main areas of what the Bootstrap people refer to as the infrastructure of the library, and provided you've tackled the basics and intent, you should have all you need in those areas of the documentation to markup pages to your heart's content. In this chapter we're just going to look at those areas so you can get a feel on where to hunt for things.

This book is by no means meant to teach you CSS basics or how to modify Bootstrap's core, rather, it's about leveraging Bootstrap from MVC. However, there are important bits you should have a feel for, especially if the idea of tinkering with Bootstrap's internals is up your alley.

 Estimated time: Less than 10 minutes

The Base CSS

Some HTML elements of the library are just "free". You get defaults for BODY, background colors, FORMS and form elements without adding any classes. for example. Others need only simple class assignment, such as styling "lead" copy on a page with the P tag.

Buttons in Bootstrap[1] use classes, which seems odd at first but they work on BUTTON, A and INPUT elements so once you learn the classes this is rather simple to apply. Each element requires the base "btn" class, and if you want additional coloring you can use one of the contextual classes (active, success, info, warning or danger).

```
1  <button type="button" class="btn btn-warning">War\
2  ning</button>
```

There are a number of scenarios where these contextual colors can be applied to backgrounds with tables or paragraphs, and be used for text as well, mostly documented in the helper classes[2] section of the site. You'll also find info on using these under component- or element-specific docs, such as with the table[3].

There is more information on the basics, as well as diving into the code for customization, on the CSS documentation page[4]. If you are familiar with SASS[5] and LESS[6], or want to trim down pieces of Bootstrap[7] that are not required for your site check out those links as well.

Bootstrap Components

When Bootstrap requires more structure to put things together you'll be looking to the component documentation. The navbar[8] we looked at yesterday, for example, needs specific containers, classes and arrangements in order for it to render properly.

---

[1] http://getbootstrap.com/css/#buttons
[2] http://getbootstrap.com/css/#helper-classes
[3] http://getbootstrap.com/css/#tables
[4] http://getbootstrap.com/css/
[5] http://getbootstrap.com/css/#sass
[6] http://getbootstrap.com/css/#less
[7] http://getbootstrap.com/getting-started/#customizing
[8] http://getbootstrap.com/components/#navbar

Dropdowns, button groups, input groups and combinations thereof are all possible with the right markup. Adding things like breadcrumbs, pagination controls, badges and labels with consistent styling has always been a thorn in my side, but they're made easy with Bootstrap.

You can dig further into these elements and more on the Components page[9].

Adding Functionality with JavaScript

It's worth noting that most everything up to this point work without the JavaScript library. However, adding the JS to your site really starts to make Bootstrap sing. (You'll also need it to handle specific use cases like navbars with collapsed regions.)

One of the things I like most about Bootstrap is that it considers the CSS markup the first-class API, meaning you don't have to write any JavaScript to make Bootstrap components like modals or tabs work. They've pushed this away into their JS file, and allow you to trigger related behaviors with data attributes, like here with the alert[10]. By simply adding a button to your alert element, you get dismiss capabilities for free:

```
1  <button type="button" class="close" data-dismiss=\
2  "alert" aria-hidden="true">&times;</button>
```

The docs on JavaScript controls[11] are a little light and don't offer much for explanation, but you can learn a fair bit by experimenting with the data attribute classes or using the JS API directly.

---

[9]http://getbootstrap.com/components/
[10]http://getbootstrap.com/javascript/#alerts
[11]http://getbootstrap.com/javascript/

Chatper 16 Summary

Knowing where to go to find out more information is great, but knowing which angle to come at it from certainly helps as well. This chapter breaks down some of conceptual aspects around Bootstrap including how things are laid out, and points you in the right direction to get help on specific aspects of the framework.

17. LESS is More: Building Bootstrap in Visual Studio

Now I know that I said that this book wasn't going to be a guide to learning LESS, but it would be a shame if I didn't at least point you in the right direction to do so. Modifying the look-and-feel of Bootstrap is straightforward, perhaps even easy, when you have the right tools. Those buttons below? Those are essentially composed of several smaller bits of color and fonts and padding and spacing to give you the look you see there. My only question is: why aren't they hot pink?

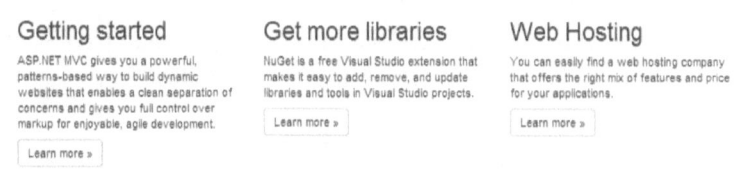

Getting started

ASP.NET MVC gives you a powerful, patterns-based way to build dynamic websites that enables a clean separation of concerns and gives you full control over markup for enjoyable, agile development.

Learn more »

Get more libraries

NuGet is a free Visual Studio extension that makes it easy to add, remove, and update libraries and tools in Visual Studio projects.

Learn more »

Web Hosting

You can easily find a web hosting company that offers the right mix of features and price for your applications.

Learn more »

The Default Styling of Buttons

Changing something simple like the color of a specific button is fine, but what about creating your own elements, or modifying the base colors of your entire layout? For this you'll need to dive into LESS. We won't go for the home run here, but we'll get to the plate and tackle that issue of the poorly-colored button.

 Estimated time: About 15 minutes

Install Web Essentials

Web Essentials[1] is one of the best add-ons that you'll add to your arsenal as a web developer. It builds on top of Browser Link features to extend your debugging and tweaking capabilities when working on HTML, CSS and JavaScript as well as other languages like CoffeeScript and TypeScript. You can think of Web Essentials as the playground where Microsoft developers go to build their wish list of things that they'd like to see in Visual Studio.

The add in has the ability to inject a tool bar into your page that makes it even easier to modify the document you're viewing and see your changes reflected in your source code (yes...edit in the browser, source code updates!).

The Web Essentials Browser Bar

It even gives you access to ZenCoding, an extension that trivializes HTML syntax and lets you write something like this:

```
1   div.row>div.col-md-3*4
```

...that automatically turns into this:

```
1   <div class="row">
2       <div class="col-md-3"></div>
3       <div class="col-md-3"></div>
4       <div class="col-md-3"></div>
5       <div class="col-md-3"></div>
6   </div>
```

---

[1]http://vswebessentials.com/

But the reason we're going to use it is because Web Essentials automatically "compiles" LESS files into CSS when you save them. Download and install[2] the latest version (you will need to restart Visual Studio).

A Playground Project

I know that the biggest reason that every developer on the planet hesitates to experiment is tied directly to cost. Every time you do **File -> New -> Project** in Visual Studio, Microsoft takes $14 from your bank account.

Wait...they don't? Perfect.

So hit **File -> New -> Project** and create a new MVC project to follow along. This chapter will use this project as a playground to modify the source of Bootstrap independent of the project we're working on in the rest of the chapters of the book.

Uninstall Bootstrap

To use our custom version of Bootstrap we're going to want to get the 'real' version out of the way. We can remove it from the list of installed packages from the Package Console Manager.

```
1   Uninstall-Package Bootstrap
```

This will take out the CSS and JavaScript that is required to use Bootstrap on your site. Don't worry...we're about to get that back.

Install Bootstrap LESS Source

Next, install the NuGet package that gives you the CSS source, called Twitter.Bootstrap.Less.

---

[2]http://vswebessentials.com/

```
1   Install-Package Twitter.Bootstrap.Less
```

This package contains the JS you need, plus the source code for Bootstrap in LESS syntax. In the Content folder, the bootstrap folder is where you'll be working with LESS.

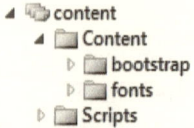

The LESS Source Package

You still don't have the CSS in your project, but we know where it's going to end up. We'll need to update our project so that we can use it when it's ready.

Update Your CSS Bundle

Whenever you make a change to a LESS file or one of its dependencies Web Essentials will generate the resultant CSS file and save it to disk in the folder where the source resides. You have two choices, you can modify the Web Essentials settings to change the output path, or you can just update the relevant bundles in your project to target the output file.

Open up BundleConfig.cs in App_Start and add the /Bootstrap directory to the path of Bootstrap.cs; this is where the file will be saved out.

```
1   bundles.Add(new StyleBundle("~/Content/css").Incl\
2   ude(
3           "~/Content/Bootstrap/bootstrap.css",
4           "~/Content/site.css"));
```

Use the Source

It's an atrocity that we now have the power to correct: those 21st century buttons need some early 1990's flair. Open up the Bootstrap.less file located in Content\Bootstrap and have a look at the includes that make up the final file.

Make a small change - perhaps add white space or your own comment - and save the file. If you then click on "Show all files" in Solution Explorer (it's one of the icons in the top bar) you will now see that Bootstrap.css file we wanted to see. Right-click on it and select "Include in Project".

Press CTRL+F5 (start without debugging) now to see the default styling with the white background and leave your browser open. It's not here yet, but this is what we want to see after our pending changes:

Getting started

ASP.NET MVC gives you a powerful, patterns-based way to build dynamic websites that enables a clean separation of concerns and gives you full control over markup for enjoyable, agile development.

Learn more »

Get more libraries

NuGet is a free Visual Studio extension that makes it easy to add, remove, and update libraries and tools in Visual Studio projects.

Learn more »

Web Hosting

You can easily find a web hosting company that offers the right mix of features and price for your applications.

Learn more »

Hot Pink Because Awesome

Now if you want to change the integral parts of the CSS classes that are compiled out from the source, you'll likely be going to the *component-name*.less file, something like Buttons.less, for example. These component files use variables to wire up templates that will compose the final Bootstrap library. But definitions of those variables used for colors, font sizes, margins and the like are actually stored in the apt-named variables.less file. Pop into that file and find the following text:

```
1   //== Buttons
```

Just below that, around line 144, is the definition of the default button styles. Update the background or bg color to the following:

```
1   @btn-default-bg:                    #fc00ff;
```

Now, save the file. You'll see a message in the status bar of Visual Studio that give you an idea about what's going on:

Compiling 1 dependent files for variables.less

Great Scott! The machine has learned!

Give it a minute to work away, then flip back to your browser. With Browser Link and Web Essentials installed, you don't even have to refresh the page...but the modified CSS output from the LESS compiler included in your CSS bundle through the MVC Framework is updated and your new, much more stylish, button appearance is reflected on the page.

Chapter 17 Summary

Some developers are blessed with rich talent in design and the ability to pull colors, fonts and spacing together to make a masterpiece of a web page, the brilliance of their efforts celebrated across the interwebs as the standard of taste and style.

I, however, am not one of those folks! But, as far as it serves this developer, there are times when it makes more sense to change a single variable or two and impact dozens or hundreds of aspects of my project.

Equipped with the LESS source of Bootstrap and the groovy Web Essentials plugin, in this chapter we explored how to modify Bootstrap's variables and change the look-and-feel of our site. We changed the package dependency so that we could access the raw code, and configured our CSS bundle to properly reference the new CSS file that was generated for us behind the scene.

IV Adding Some Sparkle

18. Customizing and Rendering Bootstrap Badges

Bootstrap comes with some great styles and base starting points, but it's not meant to be the be-all and end-all of design. There are often times when a simple CSS tweak can make your site stand apart from others. While we looked at the possibility of completely customizing Bootstrap from the ground-up in the last chapter, here we'll look at an alternate approach.

 Estimated time: About 15 minutes

Using the Built-In Badge

Badges solve the problem of relaying a bit of information to the user that something needs to be addressed, and in what kind of quantity. They are pretty easy to render, needing only a little mark up on a SPAN, using the "badge" class, and you're off to the races.

```
1   <a href="#">Registrations <span class="badge">19<\
2   /span></a>
```

That ends up looking something like this:

Bootstrap's built-in badge

And if you put it in a navbar, it looks like this:

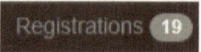

Bootstrap's built-in badge...in a navbar

So it's an easy way to convey that the user has *something* that needs to be done, check unread messages, complete some kind of task or, say, approve People registrations. But the white-on-grey is a little bland.

Non-Intrusive Customizations

> For this chapter we are returning to the main code project that we've developed throughout chapters 1-16. The side project we created in Chapter 17 does not contain the work we'll be referencing for the remainder of the book.

I wouldn't recommend modifying the base Bootstrap.css class itself in all cases. If there are incremental updates you would lose the ability to update your project without losing changes, save using a merge tool and sorting out the diff on your own. You would likely be better served to extend Bootstrap with LESS or SASS if that suits your fancy as we did in Chapter 17, but there is an easier approach as well that's as old as CSS itself: just add another stylesheet to your project. Sometimes low-tech is the easiest answer.

What we'd like to do is to get a palette of options like so:

Registrations

Oooo...pretty colors!

Let's start by adding a new CSS file to the project. Expand the Content folder in your solution and you should see bootstrap.css. Right-click on the Content folder, and add a new Style Sheet called "bootstrap.custom.css", then paste in the following code:

```
1   .badge-danger {
2      background-color: #d43f3a;
3   }
4
5   .badge-warning {
6      background-color: #d58512;
7   }
8
9   .badge-success {
10     background-color: #398439;
11  }
12
13  .badge-info {
14     background-color: #269abc;
15  }
16
17  .badge-inverse {
18     background-color: #333333;
19  }
```

These are just classes styled after the button classes, using the same solid colors for the background. You could event go a step further and introduce hover states (like buttons) or borders (like for labels) depending on your fancy.

If you did want to do this the LESS way, you would likely prefer to add these to the Badges.less file directly. This would allow you to use the variables defined for the contextual classes as the background colors in your badges.

Next, we need to get our site aware of this file. If you're a traditional web developer you might be inclined to update your template or master page and add some markup to include the CSS, but we have a different approach in today's web: update our bundle.

Including the File

Navigate to the App_Start folder in your solution and open the BundleConfig.cs file. Update the bundle that includes the bootstrap.css file to the following:

```
1  bundles.Add(new StyleBundle("~/Content/css").Incl\
2  ude(
3              "~/Content/bootstrap.css",
4              "~/Content/bootstrap.custom.css",
5              "~/Content/site.css"));
```

If you've already got the site running, you'll want to recompile at this point. You won't need to in order to make changes to your style sheet, but BundleConfig is only ever run once at startup. Bundles have built-in cachebusters that prevent your CSS from getting stale while you edit it, but you'll need to do that rebuild just once.

Cache Busting

Without making changes to your web server, one thing that has been tricky as a web developer for quite some time is getting the changes you've made and saved updated in the client. Web browsers and servers tend to do as little work as possible, so if there is any opportunity to *not* fetch a file across the wire, why do it? Thankfully, this is a solved problem. If your CSS or the configuration of your bundle changes, cache busting kicks in. It's no where near as cool as ghost busting, but you'll be thankful for it just the same. Rather than referencing a naked version of the file, you'll see something like the following in the sources that your browser requests:

http://localhost:44460/Content/css?v=8F203100AC672E09B2

The random identifier appended to the querystring at the end of the URL changes each time an update is made to relevant source files in the bundle. The changes mean the cached version of the file is invalidated and removed from memory and the server is guaranteed to return the latest version of the content on every request.

Badge Up Your Site!

Now you are free to add something like the following to any of your pages:

```
1  <p>
2      <a href="#">Registrations <span class="badge"\
3  >19</span></a>
4  </p>
```

One cool but likely expected and non-obvious aspect is that if you put a badge inside of an A tag, as I have above here, the badge is also clickable, so keep that in mind as you're hacking together your markup.

Chapter 18 Summary

Extending the CSS of Bootstrap doesn't require extra tools or Visual Studio add-ons if you're looking to add your own touch of style to your site. In this chapter we added some new classes to make our variation of Bootstrap badges pop off the page with colors that we know already work with the library.

19. Long-Running Notifications Using Badges and Entity Framework Code First

We previously looked at using `TempData` to store alerts, which is great when what we are trying to alert the user to is a transient message that lives only for the next request. What about the scenario where we have long running notifications? Unread email? Outstanding actions the user must follow up on?

In this chapter we're going to bang out a solution here...in the interest of time and simplicity some of what we do today *will not* be in line with best practices, but we'll work through some of the remaining chapters to get closer to them.

 Estimated time: Less than 20 minutes

Rocking Out A Model

If we want a way to indicate that the user needs to take care of something, we need two pieces: some kind of UI to point it out – which we have with badges – and some place to store the data – which we'll get with EF. Right click on your \Models directory and add a new class, called `Notification`, and add the following code to it:

```
1       public enum NotificationType
2       {
3           Registration,
4           Email
5       }
6
7       public class Notification
8       {
9           public int NotificationId { get; set; }
10          public string Title { get; set; }
11          public NotificationType NotificationType \
12  { get; set; }
13          public string Controller { get; set; }
14          public string Action { get; set; }
15      }
```

These are *just* classes, but when we lean on Entity Framework, we get a database out of it as well. In the "code first" approach, we first write ourselves a class that represents the data, as we've done above. Next, we have to let EF know that we expect a storage mechanism for that data, namely, we create a data context and a DB set (representing a table) inside of another class. Add SiteDataContext as a class in your Models folder and add the following code to it:

```
1       public class SiteDataContext : DbContext
2       {
3           public SiteDataContext() : base("DefaultC\
4   onnection") { }
5
6           public DbSet<Notification> Notifications \
7   { get; set; }
8       }
```

There's not much to it: DbSet represents a table and DbContext identifies this as a class that represents a connection to the database. If the DB doesn't exist, EF creates it for us. We call the base class constructor with a string, which identifies the connection string to use in the web.config file, if present, or the name of the DB that will be created if it doesn't.

At this point, **build your project** using Shift+Ctrl+B or by pressing F6. We need the app compiled to take advantage of tooling in Entity Framework.

Now, go to the Package Manager Console (View -> Other Windows -> Package Manager Console) and type the following command:

```
1  Enable-Migrations -ContextTypeName SimpleSite.Mod\
2  els.SiteDataContext
```

You'll need to make sure that the namespace and class name match what is specified above. This command generates a Configuration class that has an empty Seed method (rather, it has some comments in it, but you can delete them). This file can be used by Entity Framework as a way to do advanced configuration, set your own conventions for table naming, or, in our case, seeding the database with some test data. Paste in the following code in the Seed method:

```
1   protected override void Seed(SimpleSite.Models.Si\
2   teDataContext context)
3   {
4       context.Notifications.AddOrUpdate(notificatio\
5   n => notification.Title,
6           new Notification
7           {
8               Title = "John Smith was added to the \
9   system.",
10              NotificationType = NotificationType.R\
```

```
11   egistration
12          },
13          new Notification
14          {
15              Title = "Susan Peters was added to th\
16   e system.",
17              NotificationType = NotificationType.R\
18   egistration
19          },
20          new Notification
21          {
22              Title = "Just an FYI on Thursday's me\
23   eting",
24              NotificationType = NotificationType.E\
25   mail
26          });
27   }
```

AddOrUpdate is like an "upsert" method you can use to inject or update data in your DB. It accepts a lambda expression that specifies how unique rows are identified, and a parameter array which is a list of objects you want to inject into the specified table.

Updating our Database

With support for the migrations in place, we want to create an initial version of the DB and apply it in our development environment. From the Package Manager Console, type these lines of code:

```
1   Add-Migration db-create
2
3   Update-Database
```

Have a look through the migration class that is generated. Pretty cool, eh? Although this is just a first stab at it, it really shows how you can customize the build up – or tear down – of you tables. It's worth a whole book of content, though, so I'm not diving in for now! The call to Update-Database executes the Up() method on all outstanding migrations. Everything is tracked for you by EF in the database.

Okay, Here's One Best Practice

One thing that I really like about MVC and EF is how easy it is to get data into your view using the entities of your database. One thing that I really hate about MVC and EF is how easy it is to get data into your view using the entities of your database. For reals. It's great for demos and terrible for production.

Instead, use a view model...a way to decouple your view from your database completely. Get in this habit as early as you can, and then come back and thank me 6 months into the maintenance portion of your contract.

Add another class called NotificationViewModel and write in the following code:

```
1  public class NotificationViewModel
2  {
3      public int Count { get; set; }
4      public string NotificationType { get; set; }
5      public string BadgeClass { get; set; }
6  }
```

Rather than relying on the data in the database we're going to use a projection of the data instead. This can help to shield our UI from changes in the model and eliminate the risk of excess DB access or over-exposing sensitive data. It also allows for other best practices we'll cover in the days ahead.

Updating Our Controller

Return to your `HomeController` class and update your `Index()` action to be the following:

```
public ActionResult Index()
{
    var context = new SiteDataContext();

    var notifications = context.Notifications
        .GroupBy(n => n.NotificationType)
        .Select(g => new NotificationViewModel
        {
            Count = g.Count(),
            NotificationType = g.Key.ToString(),
            BadgeClass = NotificationType.Email =\
= g.Key
                        ? "success"
                        : "info"
        });

    ViewBag.Notifications = notifications;

    return View();
}
```

We're getting the list of notifications out of the DB, grouping them by type, specifying the style class to use and counting them up. We then set that information in the `ViewBag`, which is accessible from our views. Note that this approach *only* works for now in our Index method, and *only* on the `HomeController`. Don't worry, we'll take care of that in Chapter 20. 😊

Lighting up Notifications in the View

The navbar that is rendered throughout our site comes by way of the main layout. Open up \Views\Shared_Layout.cshtml so that we can add notification elements to our pages.

First, add the model namespace to the layout as the first line of the file:

```
1  @using SimpleSite.Models
```

Find the UL element with the class "nav navbar-nav" that contains the LI elements that compose the menu (these are around line 27 for me). At the end of the LI elements, we're going to inject a few more, so we iterate over the list of notifications that we popped into the ViewBag like so:

```
1  @foreach (NotificationViewModel notification in V\
2  iewBag.Notifications)
3  {
4      <li><a href="#">@notification.NotificationTyp\
5  e <span class="badge badge-@notification.BadgeCla\
6  ss">@notification.Count</span></a></li>
7  }
```

We've got some more work to do to fully get these working, but you will likely see the direction this is moving in by now, and users will see that something needs to be done about all those...notifications.

Our updated navigation bar

Chapter 19 - Summary (and Laments)

Well, as I said we've got some clean up to do to get a little closer to best practices. We covered a lot of ground and got some cool stuff working, but there are definitely better ways to approach some of these tasks when you're working on a real development effort.

We added models to our site to be used in conjunction with Entity Framework, but if we leave our models here they are not easily reused. I'll leave it as an exercise for you to resolve this, if you wish, by adding a new DLL project to the solution and moving your model classes there. Note that it is acceptable and advisable to create and leave view models - which are not stored in the database and usually end up being MVC-specific - right here in your web project.

We have to put code in each and every single action on every controller where we would want to see notifications. In the next chapter we'll try to clean that up a little.

Our layout is getting polluted with additional code and objectives. Many unrelated concepts are starting to be rendered in the same place, meaning it will become increasingly more difficult to maintain. We'll come back to address this in Chapter 21.

20. An `ActionFilter` to Inject Notifications

Over the last few chapters we've added some good-looking notification badges to our site using our customized Bootstrap badges. Now we need to take care of this nonsense where we need to put the same code into *every single method and every single controller* that we write.

Our Sexy Navbar with Notifications

Yay for the badges, boo for the code. To get around this, we'll explore one of many different ways we solve this problem of repeating ourselves by writing an action filter.

 Estimated time: Less than 15 minutes

A Bit About the MVC Pipeline

There's a lot going on behind the scenes in a web request, but thankfully much of it is abstracted away for most development tasks, and nearly all of it is abstracted away for the end user (could you imagine trying to explain to Mom or Dad how to manually resolve the IP address of domain name? Yikes!).

Sometimes you need to dive into the abstraction, and action filters are one area where this is the case. Remember back in Chapter 1 I broke down the request a little? And in Chapter 2 I introduced some of the MVC vernacular? Well...if you've been following along, you can probably infer what an action filter might be up to: before or after executing an action on a controller you get to inspect, prod, poke and otherwise modify the content or even redirect the user as you see fit. From MSDN[1]:

> Action filters. These implement `IActionFilter`[2] and wrap the action method execution. The `IActionFilter`[3] interface declares two methods: `OnActionExecuting`[4] and `OnActionExecuted`[5].`OnActionExecuting`[6] runs before the action method. `OnActionExecuted`[7] runs after the action method and can perform additional processing, such as providing extra data to the action method, inspecting the return value, or canceling execution of the action method.

You can deny access, restrict availability of resources and execute arbitrary code. You even have access to internal parts of MVC, so your filter can be aware of the currently executing controller, action, and target view.

And that's where we're going to hook in: just before the view is rendered, after the action method has run. If we do it ahead of the action execution we risk doing work before we know it's required (perhaps it's an unauthorized request, for example).

---

[1]http://msdn.microsoft.com/en-us/library/gg416513(vs.98).aspx

[2]http://msdn.microsoft.com/en-us/library/system.web.mvc.iactionfilter(v=vs.98).aspx

[3]http://msdn.microsoft.com/en-us/library/system.web.mvc.iactionfilter(v=vs.98).aspx

[4]http://msdn.microsoft.com/en-us/library/system.web.mvc.iactionfilter.
onactionexecuting(v=vs.98).aspx

[5]http://msdn.microsoft.com/en-us/library/system.web.mvc.iactionfilter.
onactionexecuted(v=vs.98).aspx

[6]http://msdn.microsoft.com/en-us/library/system.web.mvc.iactionfilter.
onactionexecuting(v=vs.98).aspx

[7]http://msdn.microsoft.com/en-us/library/system.web.mvc.iactionfilter.
onactionexecuted(v=vs.98).aspx

Adding the Filter

Add a folder to the root of your site called Filters (this isn't convention, just a way to help keep you organized) and then add a class called NotificationFilter. Inherit from ActionFilterAttribute, and then override the OnActionExecuted method so that you can add your two cents to the request. Your code will be nearly identical to what you put in HomeController, except note now that the ViewBag property is actually accessed through the Controller property on your filterContext.

```
public override void OnActionExecuted(ActionExecu\
tedContext filterContext)
{
    var context = new SiteDataContext();

    var notifications = context.Notifications
        .GroupBy(n => n.NotificationType)
        .Select(g => new NotificationViewModel
        {
            Count = g.Count(),
            NotificationType = g.Key.ToString(),
            BadgeClass = NotificationType.Email =\
= g.Key
                    ? "success"
                    : "info"
        });

    filterContext.Controller.ViewBag.Notification\
s = notifications;

}
```

`ActionFilterAttribute` gives you four virtual methods for actions and results on executing and executed. You only have to implement the ones that suit your fancy. Because it's an attribute class, you can decorate your actions (or even your classes) with it and the MVC Framework will pick it up and execute it when the time is right.

Touch up the Controller

Now on your `HomeController` we can clean things up a fair bit. Remove almost all the code from the `Index` action and decorate it with your new attribute.

```
1  [NotificationFilter]
2  public ActionResult Index()
3  {
4      return View();
5  }
```

Much cleaner, eh? You can now run your site and you'll get the same result as we had before, and the notifications will now appear anywhere you place that attribute. If you put it at the class level, all actions on the controller will have the filter applied. Which means I should probably mention...

...Some Notes and Caveats

This is a pretty powerful deal, especially at the class level. Heck, you can even globally register your filter and have it execute on every request. Which is why I have to stress some pretty important bits:

- If it's *always* executing, then it's *always* executing. Be mindful of decorating your classes as a rule or registering filters globally, especially if you have requests (AJAX) that maybe don't need the filter. Alternatively, design your filter in such a way that it knows when it should or shouldn't run.

- Lots-of-stuff-going-on doesn't scale well. Use filters judiciously so that you're not bogging your site down with unnecessary operations. Be vigilant in knowing if you should be filtering the request before or after action execution or view rendering. Be quick in what you do so that you return quickly and keep your performance up. Use profiling if you're not sure how fast your code is running.

- In this example – and I can get away with it because it's an example – I'm going to the database on each request. It may suit you well to do this, but consider alternate approaches (such as caches with timeouts and operations that invalidate them, or using a `CacheDependency`) so that you're not making those hits all the time.

Chapter 20 Summary

Not every request will have the prerequisites that you demand, and not all requests that enter the pipeline will require extra processing that you may wish to apply conditionally. In this chapter we had a look at home we can use components of the MVC Framework that allow us to interact with the request pipeline and make decisions about how, when and what kind of processing we want or need to address. We created a filter that accesses the database to simplify the code in our controller but were able to interact with the request at a level abstracted away from the controller itself.

21. Cleaning Up Filtering, the Layout & the Menu

In software development we often talk about concepts like the Single Responsibility Principle. Web pages are often doing *lots* of things, so it's hard to say that it should always apply when we're building our views. But, in the spirit of Martin Fowler's take on it, I would argue that our _Layout.cshtml is starting to get a lot of reasons as to why it might change, and for that reason, we're going to split out the menu.

 Estimated time: Less than 10 minutes

Extracting the Menu

In your Views\Shared folder add another partial called _MenuPartial.cshtml and paste in the following code.

```
1  @using SimpleSite.Models
2  <ul class="nav navbar-nav">
3      <li>@Html.ActionLink("Home", "Index", "Home")\
4  </li>
5      <li>@Html.ActionLink("About", "About", "Home"\
6  )</li>
7      <li>@Html.ActionLink("Contact", "Contact", "H\
8  ome")</li>
9      <li>@Html.ActionLink("My Peeps", "Index", "Si\
```

```
10  mple")</li>
11
12      @if (ViewBag.Notifications != null)
13      {
14          foreach (NotificationViewModel notificati\
15  on in ViewBag.Notifications)
16          {
17              <li>
18                  <a href="#">
19                      @notification.NotificationType
20                      <span class="badge badge-@not\
21  ification.BadgeClass">
22                          @notification.Count
23                      </span>
24                  </a>
25              </li>
26          }
27      }
28  </ul>
```

If you flip back to our _Layout view, you'll see that this is very close to what we had there. I've made two important changes:

1. I've added a link to our SimpleController in the menu.
2. I'm checking to make sure there is data in the ViewBag before accessing the dynamic property. This will prevent errors should there be no notifications for the users.

If you do #1 without #2 above at this point, you will most definitely get errors because the only place that has notifications injected is in the Index action in HomeController.

With those bits in place, be sure to pop back into your _Layout, and update the navbar where we had previously added the code for notifications. It should now only include a call to render our _MenuPartial and the _LoginPartial.

```
1  <div class="navbar-collapse collapse">
2      @Html.Partial("_MenuPartial")
3      @Html.Partial("_LoginPartial")
4  </div>
```

If you run the site at this point you won't get any errors, but you'll only see the notifications on the home page. Let's address that.

Globally Registering an Action Filter

We're now going to set it up so that our NotificationFilter is executed on every request. I just ask that you remember that this is a demo, and that there are a few caveats you should be aware of.

During application startup (checkout your global.asax in the root of the site) you'll notice a call to FilterConfig.RegisterGlobalFilters. There is no magic here. There's a static method on a class located in your App_Start folder that helps to keep that global.asax nice and tidy. A GlobalFilterCollection is passed in and we can then manipulate it as we see fit.

In previous versions of the MVC template, this wasn't around, so most folks ended up either dropping in a ton of heavy-lifting into Application_Start or otherwise coming up with a comparable solution to the above. Now, the class that does the FilterConfig does the FilterConfig. Kinda like that whole Single Responsibility Principle again, eh?

Update your FilterConfig class' static method (which has the global error handling baked in already) to also include the registration of our filter:

```
1   public static void RegisterGlobalFilters(GlobalFi\
2   lterCollection filters)
3   {
4       filters.Add(new HandleErrorAttribute());
5       filters.Add(new NotificationFilter());
6   }
```

Now, return to the HomeController and remove the NotificationFilter attribute from the Index action. It won't really matter if you don't (the Framework is smart enough to see that it's already in play) but you might confuse the future version of yourself when you disable the global registration down the road and the filter keeps getting executed.

You're all set! Try out your application now, navigating to any page to see the notification icons in the navbar.

Chapter 21 Summary

Filters can be useful at many different levels of your application, right down at the action level, for all actions on a controller, or registered up globally for all controllers or actions in your project. In this chapter we took a fairly local filter and pushed it up to the global level to get it executing on all actions. We continued our efforts to keep things simple by moving the rendering of the menu out of the layout and into it's own partial view.

V So, You've Got People Logging In

22. Sprucing up Identity for Logged In Users

Typically you wouldn't want the entirety of the internet adding and editing records at will without some form of authentication and authorization. You want to be able to keep track of who's editing your data and give your users the ability to keep track of their own.

So, let's continue with our project and build out some identity capabilities.

 Estimated time: Less than 20 minutes

Okay, I'm Kidding. Just Press F5!

Great work, you're all done!

As most folks are well aware, the default templates for Asp.Net applications now ship with a sample account administration implementation (reasonably good ones, at that). Users are able to register and log in using pre-built models, controllers and views. You can easily extend the template with 3rd party login capabilities, allowing folks with Microsoft, Facebook or Google accounts (and, and, and...) to log into your site as well. We've now got substantial improvements to identity management overall, with things like two-factor authentication, reductions in the leaky abstractions we've lived with for some time, better testability, more flexibility in storage options, and more.

If you're not familiar with these bits, it's worth having a look, **but this is a topic already well covered**. Believe me, if you're going to be working with user accounts and registration on your site these articles are all worth the reads:

- The Asp.Net Identity web site[1]
- A background article on Identity[2] by the Asp.Net team
- Two-Factor authentication[3] with SMS
- Using third-party authentication providers[4] on your site (Facebook, Twitter, Google, LinkedIn)

But we're here to do Bootstrappy things, right? So let's spruce up that top bar a little for our logged in users with some MVC bits we build (HTML helpers) and some Bootstrap bits (image classes) that will take our site up a level.

Bootstrap Image Classes

The CSS library gives us a few easy-to-use helpers to make our images look consistent. Here's a sample from the Bootstrap site[5]:

---

[1] http://www.asp.net/identity
[2] http://www.asp.net/identity/overview/getting-started/introduction-to-aspnet-identity
[3] http://www.asp.net/identity/overview/features-api/two-factor-authentication-using-sms-and-email-with-aspnet-identity
[4] http://www.asp.net/mvc/tutorials/mvc-5/create-an-aspnet-mvc-5-app-with-facebook-and-google-oauth2-and-openid-sign-on
[5] http://getbootstrap.com/css/#images

I actually failed 'circles' in kindergarten

The classes are as follows:

- `img-rounded` – provides rounded corners to your rectangular images
- `img-circle` – turns any image into a circle
- `img-thumbnail` – makes your image look like a little Polaroid of itself

Making Members Feel Welcome

Today we're just going to add a little touch to the navbar that our logged in users will see, keying in off of the default implementation of the Identity providers. We'll head in that direction by extending our `HtmlHelper` that generates Gravatar images, as we need to add a property for a CSS class to give us a nice round face on the page. But first, we'll have to add the following line of code to the `GravatarOptions` class:

```
1  public string CssClass { get; set; }
```

We'll need to add that to the tag, so let's revist the `GravatarImage`, likely located in the Helpers folder, to check for a value and add it to the tag if present. The full method should now look like this:

```
1   public static HtmlString GravatarImage(this HtmlH\
2   elper htmlHelper, string emailAddress, GravatarOp\
3   tions options = null)
4   {
5       if (options == null)
6           options = GravatarOptions.GetDefaults();
7
8       var imgTag = new TagBuilder("img");
9
10      emailAddress = string.IsNullOrEmpty(emailAddr\
11  ess) ? string.Empty : emailAddress.Trim().ToLower\
12  ();
13
14      // <-- adding support for CSS
15      if (!string.IsNullOrEmpty(options.CssClass))
16      {
17          imgTag.AddCssClass(options.CssClass);
18      }
19      // adding support for CSS  -->
20
21      imgTag.Attributes.Add("src",
22          string.Format("http://www.gravatar.com/av\
23  atar/{0}?s={1}{2}{3}",
24              GetMd5Hash(emailAddress),
25              options.Size,
26              "&d=" + options.DefaultImageType,
27              "&r=" + options.RatingLevel
28              )
29          );
30
31      return new HtmlString(imgTag.ToString(TagRend\
32  erMode.SelfClosing));
33  }
```

Unfortunately there isn't quite the exact Bootstrap class we need to make our image place and size well in the navbar, so we'll need to open up our bootstrap.custom.css file and add the following structural class:

```
1  .navbar-image {
2    float: left;
3    padding: 10px 5px;
4  }
```

Finally, we'll pop over to our _LoginPartial.cshtml (in Views\Shared) and modify the block of code displayed for logged in users. Because I'm reusing the user's name a couple of times (which is also their email address) I'm storing it in a variable first, and using that throughout the block. I also add a DIV as a container for our image, using the class that we just created. Last, I make a call to our GravatarImage helper, passing in the username (email!), an appropriate size for the toolbar (30px), and the Bootstrap class that gives us the shape we're looking for (img-circle).

```
1  var username = User.Identity.GetUserName();
2  using (Html.BeginForm("LogOff", "Account", FormMe\
3  thod.Post, new { id = "logoutForm", @class = "nav\
4  bar-right" }))
5  {
6
7  @Html.AntiForgeryToken()
8
9  <div class="navbar-image">
10     @Html.GravatarImage(username, new GravatarOpt\
11 ions { Size = 30, CssClass = "img-circle" })
12 </div>
13
14 <ul class="nav navbar-nav navbar-right">
```

```
15      <li>
16          @Html.ActionLink("Hello " + username + "!\
17  ", "Manage", "Account", routeValues: null, htmlAt\
18  tributes: new { title = "Manage" })
19      </li>
20      <li><a href="javascript:document.getElementBy\
21  Id('logoutForm').submit()">Log off</a></li>
22  </ul>
23  }
```

And now we're rockin' head shots in our navbar!

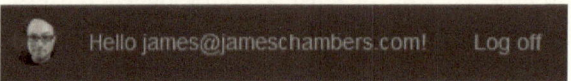

What a handsome young man

Perhaps you've modified your user profiles so that the username doesn't have to be an email address. You could easily modify this example to read from a different property and generate the same type of effect.

Chapter 22 Summary

Simple touches can help to build engagement with your users. In this chapter we enhanced a couple of our classes to assist with rendering Gravatars and jazz up our navbar. We used Bootstrap's image classes to turn the otherwise square Gravatar into a circle on the fly. We put this all together by modifying the source of the partial that renders the user login UI and started displaying Gravatars based on the logged-in user's email address.

23. Choosing Your Own Look-And-Feel

Here's the thing: everybody's site is going to look the same if everybody's site uses Bootstrap, right? Well, if we did that to users, we'd sure be missing the point as developers, and for two key reasons:

1. With the LESS and SASS source it's easy to customize, and
2. Because it's easy to customize, there's already people creating all kinds of alternate themes for Bootstrap.

So, we aren't headed down a slippery slope here, we just need to make a little effort to give our users some unique looking sites. Other posts will show you how to replace the Bootstrap theme, but this one will show you how to let your users choose from a list you've pre-built.

 Estimated time: Less than 20 minutes

Download a Free Substitute

There are some great, free alternatives located at Bootswatch.com[1]. So, start there and pick one or two to download, I chose Amelia and Darkly. We need to create a folder structure to organize our themes,

---

[1]http://bootswatch.com/

and move the CSS into those folders. Mine ended up working like this:

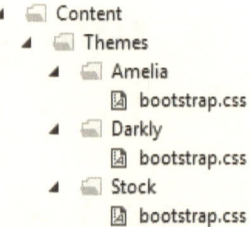

The folder structure for themes

Note that I also pushed a copy of the stock CSS for bootstrap into this structure. This allows us to simplify our code for theme switching, allowing users to pick the base theme if they like.

> **Shameless plug**: If you're looking for professionally designed themes to replace your palette, you can help out this blogger (me!) by purchasing one over at {wrap}bootstrap[a]. They have a selection of great looking Bootstrap themes. A very affordable alternative to taking the time to create your own theme.
>
> ———————
> [a]https://wrapbootstrap.com/?ref=BootstrapOnMvc

Creating a Helper Class

Next, we create a class called Bootstrap.cs (I put mine in \Helpers) so that we can programmatically work with the themes. This class is responsible for presenting the list of supported themes and resolving the path to them when we try to load the bundles.

```
1   public class Bootstrap
2   {
3       public const string BundleBase = "~/Content/c\
4   ss/";
5
6       public class Theme
7       {
8           public const string Stock = "Stock";
9           public const string Amelia = "Amelia";
10          public const string Darkly = "Darkly";
11      }
12
13      public static HashSet<string> Themes = new Ha\
14  shSet<string>
15      {
16          Theme.Stock,
17          Theme.Amelia,
18          Theme.Darkly
19      };
20
21      public static string Bundle(string themename)
22      {
23          return BundleBase + themename;
24      }
25  }
```

This is a simple class, but it prevents us from duplicating code all over the place or unnecessary spelling mistakes.

The other nice thing is that if you choose to add another theme to your project, you will just have to modify this one file and the rest will fall into place. For that to happen, we'll need to modify our startup to generate all the appropriate bundles.

Updating Our Startup Bits

Head into BundleConfig.cs (inside of \App_Startup) and replace the code that creates the Bootstrap bundle with the following:

```
1   foreach (var theme in Bootstrap.Themes)
2   {
3       var stylePath = string.Format("~/Content/Them\
4   es/{0}/bootstrap.css", theme);
5
6       bundles.Add(new StyleBundle(Bootstrap.Bundle(\
7   theme)).Include(
8                   stylePath,
9                   "~/Content/bootstrap.custom.css",
10                  "~/Content/site.css"));
11  }
```

We're simply looping over that handle collection we created so that we could generate a bundle for every installed theme. We always want all the themes – startup is only run at as the application starts, so we need them all there – as different users may wish to select different themes.

Making Our Layout "Themeable"

What we really need to do here is just a quick update to figure out the user's current theme, and then figure out what the correct bundle to use is. Update the code in _Layout to do so as follows:

```
1  @{
2      var theme = Session["CssTheme"] as string ?? \
3  Bootstrap.Theme.Stock;
4  }
5  @Styles.Render(Bootstrap.Bundle(theme))
```

I'm using Session for now, but I'll explain why in a bit that is bad idea. 😊

Note that, at this point, you could set that theme default – right now set to Bootstrap.Theme.Stock – to whichever theme you like and run your app. The mechanics of building the bundle and the class to resolve it are all in place.

Letting the User Choose a Theme

Once again we're going to revisit the _LoginPartial.cshtml file (in Views\Shared). In this round, we're going to update the text that shows the logged in user's email address (which, by default, is also their username). The LI for the username is now going to be a dropdown box in the navbar.

```
1  <li class="dropdown">
2      <a href="#" class="dropdown-toggle" data-togg\
3  le="dropdown">Hello @username! <span class="caret\
4  "></span></a>
5      <ul class="dropdown-menu" role="menu">
6          <li>
7              @Html.ActionLink("Manage Account", "M\
8  anage", "Account", routeValues: null, htmlAttribu\
9  tes: new { title = "Manage" })
10         </li>
11         <li class="divider"></li>
12         @foreach (var theme in Bootstrap.Themes)
```

```
13            {
14                <li><a href="@Url.Action("ChangeTheme\
15    ", "Profile", new { themename = theme})">@theme</\
16    a></li>
17            }
18        </ul>
19    </li>
```

I've taken that LI that was there – all it had was the user name, which was a link to Manage Account – and replaced it will all of the above code. We put in a divider and iterate over the list of known themes. Each will be a link to a ChangeTheme action on the ProfileController.

Adding our New Profile Controller

Throw ProfileController.cs in your \Controllers directory with the following, lone action in the class:

```
1    public ActionResult ChangeTheme(string themename)
2    {
3        Session["CssTheme"] = themename;
4        if (Request.UrlReferrer != null)
5        {
6            var returnUrl = Request.UrlReferrer.ToStr\
7    ing();
8            return new RedirectResult(returnUrl);
9        }
10        return RedirectToAction("Index", "Home");
11    }
```

If we have a referring URL we can push the user back to the same page, otherwise we ship them home. The preference of theme is set in the Session.

And there you have it: users can now pick their own theme on your site:

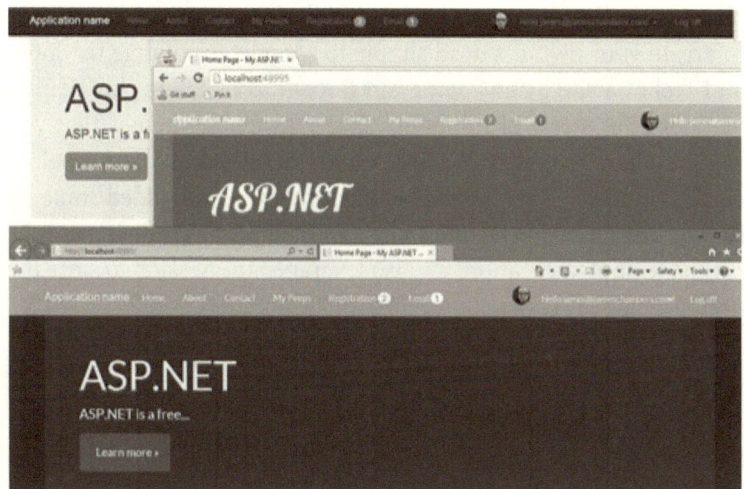

Different themes rendered after a user's selection

Why This Misses the Awesome

This data doesn't really belong in the user's session...whenever the app pool is recycled or the website or IIS is restarted or their session expires they will lose the theme choice they make. Even worse, session and Identity aren't on the same lifecycle, so when they log out the session persists and they'll still see the theme they chose when they logged in.

So that has some awesomeness deficiencies for sure, and we already have a better vehicle for storing user-related data: our database. We'll address this issue in our next chapter.

Chapter 23 Summary

Should you choose to adopt someone else's variant of Bootstrap or to create your own it's dead simple to completely change the look-and-feel of a site by swapping out Bootstrap's CSS. In this chapter we looked at a few of the tamer, freely-available themes that you can drop into your site with little effort. We also added some helper classes to more easily switch between themes, and added some UI so that users could make the switch on their own. While it's not the complete implementation, we also leveraged the Session to store the user's choice of theme.

24. Storing User Profile Information

Session is an attractive and oft-used mechanism for storing user profile data. It's freely available and has been around forever. But session state and logged-in user identity, while they may seem closely related, do not operate on the same lifecycle and sensitive data, personal data, could get "leaked out".

This post assumes you've been following along with the code in previous chapters, but more importantly that you have already signed in at least once with a registered user. You can load the chapter's source from the Git branch if you haven't, and then register a new user.

 Estimated time: About 15 minutes

A Better Place to Store User Profile Data

In Chapter 23 we penned in the user's choice of Bootstrap Theme and stored their selection in the Session object. Brock Allen wrote a great post[1] a couple years back on why this kind of thing isn't a great approach. The things that concern us most are that:

---

[1]http://brockallen.com/2012/04/07/think-twice-about-using-session-state/

- By default, session isn't durable and doesn't scale
- Even if we move to a more durable session management approach, there's no persistence of session data and yet we're making network hops
- Session isn't tied to users signing in or out

So, today, we're going to fix that Session access with a permanent, more reliable and secure approach.

Extending the User Profile Data

Since you've already created an account, you technically have some profile information already stored in your site's database. We're going to leverage the identity infrastructure of our project and extend the class that keeps track of our data, adding in the user's selected theme. In your Solution Explorer, locate the ApplicationUser class under Models. The easiest way is usually just through the search box at the top:

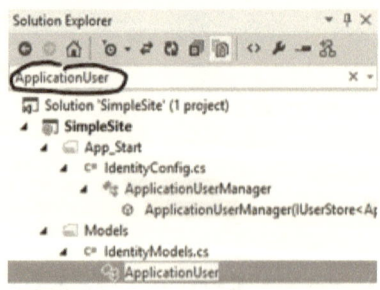

Using search in Solution Explorer

Add the following property to your ApplicationUser class:

```
1  public string CssTheme { get; set; }
```

Something to keep in mind: we're going to be modifying a class that participates in Entity Framework persistence, as managed by the Asp.Net Identity libraries. This is handy, but not free. Because we're changing essentially the schema of a table, we'll also need to enable and create a migration from the Package Manager Console:

```
1  Enable-Migrations -ContextTypeName SimpleSite.Mod\
2  els.ApplicationDbContext -MigrationsDirectory Mig\
3  rations\Identity
4  Add-Migration CssTheme -ConfigurationTypeName Sim\
5  pleSite.Migrations.Identity.Configuration
```

Note that we've got a pre-existing migration on our site, **so we need to now be more specific** and explicitly name the Configuration type. Also, in enabling the migrations, I added the MigrationsDirectory folder for the DbContext, so that our identity-related migrations would be in a sub-folder.

The Entity Framework created the appropriate classes for me to track DbContext-specific settings and the migration that I needed to update the database, but those are just the classes, nothing's changed in the DB yet. That all needs to be followed by an update to our database like so:

```
1  Update-Database -ConfigurationTypeName SimpleSite\
2  .Migrations.Identity.Configuration
```

We can now store the data we need to, we just need a way to be able to stuff it in there.

Updating our Controller

Since we're now targeting a user managed from the Identity libraries we're going to wipe out the code that writes to session and instead use the relevant classes to locate the user profile and update it. Head over to ProfileController.cs (in Helpers\) and replace the call to Session with the following:

```
1  var userStore = new UserStore<ApplicationUser>(ne\
2  w ApplicationDbContext());
3  var manager = new UserManager<ApplicationUser>(us\
4  erStore);
5  var user = manager.FindById(User.Identity.GetUser\
6  Id());
7  user.CssTheme = themename;
8  manager.Update(user);
```

And remember to import the required namespaces:

```
1  using Microsoft.AspNet.Identity;
2  using Microsoft.AspNet.Identity.EntityFramework;
3  using SimpleSite.Models;
```

We resolve the user through a UserManager, and the manager needs a UserStore to locate it's data. We can then set the CssTheme and update the user through the manager. ApplicationUser and ApplicationDbContext are just the names of the types that were automatically created for you through the project template.

Updating our Layout

Open up _Layout.cshtml (in Shared\Views) and update the code that resolves the correct style bundle. Start by adding a few using statements to the top of the view:

```
1  @using Microsoft.AspNet.Identity
2  @using Microsoft.AspNet.Identity.EntityFramework
```

We're going to use a similar approach to what we did in the controller to find the user and property, and we'll handle the null case a little differently than we were previously as well by setting the default in advance.

```
1  @{
2      var theme = Bootstrap.Theme.Stock;
3      if (User.Identity.IsAuthenticated)
4      {
5          var userStore = new UserStore<Application\
6  User>(new ApplicationDbContext());
7          var manager = new UserManager<Application\
8  User>(userStore);
9          var user = manager.FindById(User.Identity\
10 .GetUserId());
11         theme = user.CssTheme ?? theme;
12     }
13     @Styles.Render(Bootstrap.Bundle(theme))
14 }
```

Our other line of code – to actually render the bundle – will remain the same, as you can see at the bottom.

Wait, What Did We Actually Do Again?

I know, I know, it's hard to put time into something when it seems that nothing really changed. Our functionality is identical and users still have the same options as they did before.

Users can select a theme as before

But technically our solution is a little more sound. Here's what we did again as a bit of a recap:

- We added a CssTheme property to our ApplicationUser class
- We enabled migrations on our ApplicationDbContext, using a specify folder for our identity migrations
- We added a migration to accommodate our new CssTheme property
- We updated our controller to use the Identity objects instead of Session
- We refactored our _Layout to get the theme of choice from the user's profile information

For brownie points here, one could likely go to the "manage" bits (under Controllers\AccountController and Views\Account) and allow the user to make a theme selection from there. It's likely a better home than continuously being available from the home page.

Chapter 24 Summary

Session has served developers on the ASP and ASP.NET stack for the better part of two decades, but times have changed, and so have the technologies that support us and the types of applications we're building. In this chapter we extended the classes that define a user profile and moved the user's theme preference out of the `Session` and into the database. We created the appropriate migration scripts and updated our layout to look for the property in the user's profile information.

25. Personalizing Notifications

Back in Chapter 19 we introduced persistent storage for notifications, allowing us to pop a custom badge up in the navbar. This was great, but as we left it, it was creating notifications only in the Seed method of our DbContext migrations configuration, and the notifications were shown to all users. Not too helpful for dialing in on specific details or messages for specific users.

Today we're going to get that "everyone's data" out of the mix, update our notifications so that they belong to a single user and then create a temporary way for us to add new, user-specific notifications to the site.

 Estimated time: Less than 15 minutes

Clearing our DB and Seed Method

Let's get those records (from our Seed method) out of the database. Locate your DB in SQL Server Management Studio and delete the rows. Something this simple is adequate:

```
1   delete from notifications
```

Remember that effort of removing those rows is in vain if we don't clean out our Seed method as well. Each time the database configuration class is used to perform or check for migrations it will re-insert those rows.

Locate the `Configuration` class, which should be in \Migrations directory in the root of your solution. Comment out or delete all the code we added to upsert the notifications.

Extend our Notifications Class

Let's next add a couple of properties to our `Notification` class, located in \Models.

```
1   public string UserId { get; set; }
2   public bool IsDismissed { get; set; }
```

When we modify a class that takes part in Entity Framework database access that we'll also need to generate a migration and update the database to match our model. Type these commands into the Package Manager Console, updating the namespace appropriately for your project:

```
1   Add-Migration PersonalNotifications -Configuratio\
2   nTypeName SimpleSite.Migrations.Configuration
3   Update-Database -ConfigurationTypeName SimpleSite\
4   .Migrations.Configuration
```

The first command creates a migration for us, and the second updates the database accordingly.

Updating our `ActionFilter`

When we were developing the `NotificationFilter` I mentioned that at every take we should be doing as much as possible to do as little as possible. If notifications belong only to known users then we never want our filter to execute if the current request is for an unauthenticated visitor to our site. We'll also want to make sure that we only capture notifications for the user that is currently logged in, and then, only the notifications that have not yet been marked as dismissed.

The class file will need the following using statement added:

```
1  using Microsoft.AspNet.Identity;
```

Here's the updated code for the NotificationFilter (located in \Filters):

```
1  public override void OnActionExecuted(ActionExecu\
2  tedContext filterContext)
3  {
4      if (!filterContext.HttpContext.User.Identity.\
5  IsAuthenticated) return;
6
7      var userId = filterContext.HttpContext.User.I\
8  dentity.GetUserId();
9
10     var context = new SiteDataContext();
11     var notifications = context.Notifications
12         .Where(n => n.UserId == userId)
13         .Where(n => !n.IsDismissed)
14         .GroupBy(n => n.NotificationType)
15         .Select(g => new NotificationViewModel
16         {
17             Count = g.Count(),
18             NotificationType = g.Key.ToString(),
19             BadgeClass = NotificationType.Email =\
20  = g.Key
```

```
21                    ? "success"
22                    : "info"
23          });
24
25      filterContext.Controller.ViewBag.Notification\
26  s = notifications;
27  }
```

Scaffolding a Temporary Controller and View

The MVC Framework has some great scaffolding capabilities, as we've explored in minor detail so far. Today we're going to use this feature to create an entire controller and the related views for all our CRUD operations. Right-click as you normally do on the controllers folder, and click Add -> Controller.

This time 'round, use the scaffold for the "MVC5 Controller with views, using Entity Framework". Fill out the options as follows:

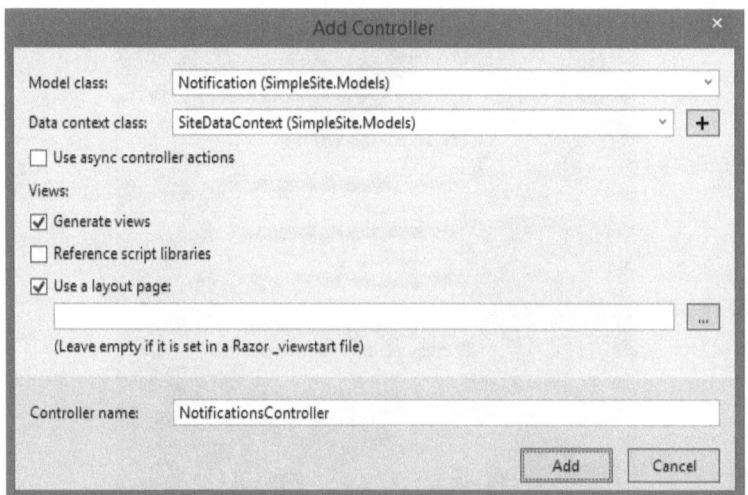

Scaffolding a controller with actions and related views

You are selecting the Notification model, checking off "Generate views" and "Use a layout page". The controller name should automatically be set to NotificationsController for you. Click Add to finish it out, and then you can navigate to this new part of your site by going to, for example, /Notifications/Create in your browser.

The scaffolded create view

One more thing: you're going to want an easy way to get your
UserId – it's what we're using to match the notifications – so add
the following to your Create view in Views\Notifications\Create.cshtml:

```
1  @if (User.Identity.IsAuthenticated)
2  {
3      <p>Your User ID is <b>@User.Identity.GetUserI\
4  d()</b></p>
5  }
```

That will output your UserId (which is a Guid) so that you can create
notifications for yourself as you can see above. Any notifications
that you create without that exact Guid will not be visible to you in
the navbar when you log in.

Now when you run the site, sign in and navigate to the /Notifica-
tions path. This will show you an empty list, but you'll have a link to
create some new records. Add some to the site, using your UserId,
and watch the navbar light up.

Navbar 2.0, now with notifications for reals!

Some Notes on this Approach

Now, I did say this is a temporary solution. By no means would you actually have a situation where you'd have users enter their own notifications, you'd more likely have events happen in the system that require some notification to be required – perhaps the completion of a job or a required update to some business process.

That's why we just used the scaffolding today...the Notification-sController and view are something that you'll likely eventually just delete...and that's okay! One of the nice things about scaffolding is that you're not married to it. So delete it when you're done with it.

In the real world, however, you would likely want users to be able to see and manage notifications in some way. We'll unpack that over the next couple of chapters.

Chapter 25 Summary

In this chapter we revisited our implementation of notifications and made them user-centric. To do this, we had to clear out the previous notifications in the database and the seed code that was generating them automatically. We updated the filter that runs on every request to our site so that it was only entrant if the site visitor was logged in, and it only returns notifications for the current user. Finally, we scaffolded out a controller, some actions and the related views using the MVC tooling, and added an easy way for the logged in user to create notifications they could see in the navbar.

26. Bootstrap Tabs for Managing Accounts

We've got this notification thing going on now and we'd like to give users a way to review notifications. There's a fairly acceptable landing spot on the "Manage Account" view (at /Account/Manage in your browser), at least for the purpose of these exercises, so we'll flesh things out there.

However, the view is isn't really set up for notifications (it's truthfully not the best spot) so we'll need to give us some UI to make it work.

 Estimated time: About 10 minutes

Understanding the Tab Component

There are two main elements you'll need to get the tabs going correctly, a UL tag that will set up as the menu elements, and a DIV to act as a container for the content.

```
1  <ul class="nav nav-tabs" role="tablist" id="accou\
2  ntTab">
3    <!-- content -->
4  </ul>
5
6  <div class="tab-content">
7    <!-- content -->
8  </div>
```

Visually, you can link those elements as illustrated below:

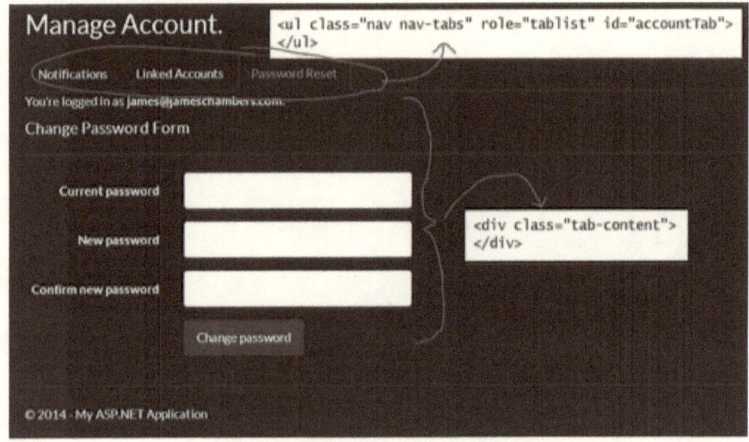

Markup related to the rendering of tabs

Because our site includes the JavaScript library for Bootstrap our tabs will automatically render and behave correctly. The classes help with the visuals, and the JS takes care of the behavior.

The UL will contain LI elements for each tab that you wish to display on the page. For us, that will the notifications, linked accounts and password reset. Those last two are the content that already exists on the page at \Views\Account\Manage.cshtml, and the notifications bits are what we'll fill in after our tabs are in place.

In addition to those two root elements, you can use a bit of JavaScript to manipulate the tabs if needed. For example, if you wanted a particular tab displayed on page load, you could use the ID as part of a jQuery selector and call the show method as follows:

```
1  $('#accountTab a[href="#linkedAccounts"]').tab('s\
2  how');
```

The DIV for content will in turn hold container elements for the rest of the content you want on the page. The structure will look something like this:

```
1  <div class="tab-content">
2      <div class="tab-pane active" id="notification\
3  s">
4          <!-- content -->
5      </div>
6      <div class="tab-pane" id="linkedAccounts">
7          <!-- content -->
8      </div>
9      <div class="tab-pane" id="passwordReset">
10         <!-- content -->
11     </div>
12 </div>
```

Each of the tab-pane DIVs could also have a fade class applied, which creates a nice content-switching visual. Let's use that.

Updating the View

If you haven't done so already, open up the \Views\Account\Manage.cshtml file and start cutting it up!

Inside the DIV.row DIV.col-md-12 structure, add the UL for the
tab headers, and add a DIV to contain the tab pages including a
placeholder for notifications, and the DIVs for linked accounts and
password reset. Move the content from those parts of the page in.

The final page code should be similar to the following:

```
1   @using SimpleSite.Models;
2   @using Microsoft.AspNet.Identity;
3   @{
4       ViewBag.Title = "Manage Account";
5   }
6
7   <h2>@ViewBag.Title.</h2>
8
9   <div class="row">
10      <div class="col-md-12">
11          <p class="text-success">@ViewBag.StatusMe\
12  ssage</p>
13
14          <ul class="nav nav-tabs" role="tablist" i\
15  d="accountTab">
16              <li class="active"><a href="#notifica\
17  tions" role="tab" data-toggle="tab">Notifications\
18  </a></li>
19              <li><a href="#linkedAccounts" role="t\
20  ab" data-toggle="tab">Linked Accounts</a></li>
21              <li><a href="#passwordReset" role="ta\
22  b" data-toggle="tab">Password Reset</a></li>
23          </ul>
24
25          <div class="tab-content">
26
27              <div class="tab-pane fade active" id=\
```

```
28   "notifications">
29                    <p>Here's where we'll put our not\
30   ifications.</p>
31            </div>
32
33            <div class="tab-pane fade" id="linked\
34   Accounts">
35                <section id="externalLogins">
36                    @Html.Action("RemoveAccountLi\
37   st")
38                    @Html.Partial("_ExternalLogin\
39   sListPartial", new ExternalLoginListViewModel { A\
40   ction = "LinkLogin", ReturnUrl = ViewBag.ReturnUr\
41   l })
42                </section>
43            </div>
44
45            <div class="tab-pane fade" id="passwo\
46   rdReset">
47                @if (ViewBag.HasLocalPassword)
48                {
49                    @Html.Partial("_ChangePasswor\
50   dPartial")
51                }
52                else
53                {
54                    @Html.Partial("_SetPasswordPa\
55   rtial")
56                }
57            </div>
58
59        </div>
60    </div>
61 </div>
```

```
62
63
64   @section Scripts { @Scripts.Render("~/bundles/jqu\
65   eryval") }
```

This leaves us with a tabbed layout, ready for our notifications to be loaded into the interface. Navigate to Account/Manage to see your handiwork. All that's left now is to get our list of user-specific notifications into our view. In the next chapter we'll get a view model figured out, populate it with the user's notifications and get it rendering in a Bootstrap-styled table in the view.

Chapter 26 Summary

We have a lot of choices for how we're going to render content and user interface in our applications, and tabs are just one of several options for doing so. In the chapter we examined the markup required by Bootstrap to put tabs together and moved our existing content from the view inside. We also added a placeholder for our notifications, which we'll address next.

27. Rendering Data in a Bootstrap Table

We created a nice tab for our users to be able to manage the different components of their account, hi-jacking the Manage Account feature of the default MVC template. Now we want to render the user's outstanding notifications in a good looking table in one of those tabs.

> **Caution:** this is the *lipstick on a pig* post of the series. Here be dragons...

 Estimated time: About 20 minutes

Rendering Tables with Bootstrap

The first thing you need to know is that you don't have to throw away a single thing you've learned in your years of HTML ninja skill building. Tables are still not to be used for layout. Tables are for lists of data. And more importantly, Bootstrap doesn't try to change the semantics or document structure for a table. In fact, to get the Bootstrap look-and-feel in an HTML table, you need to apply but one class.

```
1  <table class="table">
2    ...
3  </table>
```

So what else does it offer? A bunch of common things that you might try to do, like "tighter[1]" versions of a table, striped styling[2] or hover-states[3]. You can also use the now familiar contextual classes[4] on rows or cells to highlight pertinent information to your users.

All in all, it's a clean looking table that will suit most needs and fit in with the rest of the site.

An example of a Bootstrap-styled table

Another important aspect of the Bootstrap table is the ability to easily make a table responsive. At first, I didn't have the answer as to why this isn't the default, but it's easily added with a DIV wrapper that has the table-responsive class. This adds horizontal scroll bars to your tables, when needed, when they are viewed on smaller screens to ensure that the data doesn't end up in some non-accessible, off-device part of the screen.

---

[1] http://getbootstrap.com/css/#tables-condensed
[2] http://getbootstrap.com/css/#tables-striped
[3] http://getbootstrap.com/css/#tables-hover-rows
[4] http://getbootstrap.com/css/#tables-contextual-classes

Type	Notification	Actic
Registration	foo	
Registration	asdfa	
Email	asdfasdf	
Email	Asdfasefasef	
Email	aefasefasef	

Tables are made responsive with a simple wrapper

That wrapper looks like the following:

```
1  <div class="table-responsive">
2      <table class="table table-striped ">
3          <!-- table rows here -->
4      </table>
5  </div>
```

From there, it becomes more clear as to why the responsive table isn't the default. If you look at the image of the responsive table above - with the scroll bar - it's obvious that a container is required to get scrolling in place. In fact, if you dive into the Bootstrap source, you'll see it spelled out quite clearly inside of the media query for smaller device widths, dropping hints to the browser on overflow, scrollbars, and touch:

```
1  .table-responsive {
2    width: 100%;
3    margin-bottom: 15px;
4    overflow-x: auto;
5    overflow-y: hidden;
6    -webkit-overflow-scrolling: touch;
7    -ms-overflow-style: -ms-autohiding-scrollbar;
8    border: 1px solid #ddd;
9  }
```

It even goes further, removing wrapping, margins and borders for cells and headers. So, yes, there is great purpose in that outer container and we can't get it for free with the TABLE element.

Retrieving the Notifications

We're going to need to get the list of notifications that haven't yet been dismissed. You may have already created some test data with the efforts from the past few chapters, and that will work great here.

Open the AccountController class and navigate down to the Manage action. Just before it, add the following code :

```
1   private IEnumerable<Notification> GetUserNotifica\
2   tions()
3   {
4       // get the user ID
5       var userId = User.Identity.GetUserId();
6
7       // load our notifications
8       var context = new SiteDataContext();
9       var notifications = context.Notifications
10          .Where(n => n.UserId == userId)
11          .Where(n => !n.IsDismissed)
```

```
12          .Select(n => n)
13          .ToList();
14      return notifications;
15  }
```

All this guy is doing, really, is snapping up the rows for this currently logged in user.

One thing to mention here is that we're really now *crying* for some Dependency Injection. Our `NotificationFilter` and our `AccountController` are now both creating instances of our `SiteDataContext` – now multiple instances per request – and it's making our code harder to test.

Adding the Data to Our ViewBag

Both the GET and POST versions of `Manage` are already relying on `ViewBag` to get data up to the view, so we'll follow the same cue and put our notifications in there. In both methods you'll find the `ReturnUrl` being assigned to a `ViewBag` property, so immediately after that, add the following line of code:

```
1   ViewBag.NotificationList = GetUserNotifications();
```

Adding a Partial View for the Table

Next, let's get a partial view added called "_RenderNotifications.cshtml. The model type for the page will be a `IEnumerable<Notification>`, and we'll iterate over the collection of rows to generate the TR and relevant TDs inside each of those. The entire view will look something like this:

```
1  @using SimpleSite.Models
2  @model IEnumerable<Notification>
3
4  <div class="table-responsive">
5      <table class="table table-striped ">
6          <tr>
7              <th>Type</th>
8              <th>Notification</th>
9              <th>Actions</th>
10          </tr>
11          @foreach (var notification in Model)
12          {
13              var badgeClass = NotificationType.Ema\
14  il == notification.NotificationType
15                  ? "label-success"
16                  : "label-info";
17              <tr>
18                  <td><span class="label @badgeClas\
19  s">@notification.NotificationType</span></td>
20                  <td>@notification.Title</td>
21                  <td></td>
22              </tr>
23          }
24      </table>
25  </div>
```

There's a placeholder in there for "Actions", which we'll look at in Chapter 28 when we revisit buttons and explore drop-downs.

Updating our Manage View

With the partial view in place and the data being loaded into the ViewBag we're ready to update our view. Return to the Manage.cshtml file and locate our placeholder for the notifications.

Update it to render the partial view, passing in the collection of notifications.

```
1  <div class="tab-pane active" id="notifications">
2      @Html.Partial("_RenderNotifications", ViewBag\
3  .NotificationList as IEnumerable<Notification>)
4  </div>
```

That should be it! Viewing the page in your browser should reveal the fruits of your effort.

> I seem to have found what looks like a bug in Bootstrap, you may see this as well in your work. If you have a table in a tab, and the tab is set to active and you have applied the fade class, the table doesn't seem to be visible on page load. It shows up fine after clicking on a tab, but to work around this you'll notice that I've removed the fade class from the tab.

Oh Noes! It's Turned Into A Mess!

Folks, I'm not going to lie; though the AccountController and Manage views may have never have been intended to handle our humble little notifications, I found several things in both the controller and related views that left me uncomfortable with the design. I'm trying to keep this as a "how to get some MVC in your Bootstrap" type series, but all of the following were worth noting as things I'd try to avoid:

- Nested views with non-obvious dependencies
- Multiple methods that do the same work as each other
- Magic strings

- Methods doing too many things or things that you wouldn't attribute of them by their name (for example, the "Manage" action which resolves status messages based on optional parameters)
- `ViewBag` use that gets in the way of the view's maintainability
- Views that don't leverage Bootstrap enough
- Way too much reliance on `ViewBag`, and, therefore,
- Absence of reasonable view models
- Dogs and cats playing together

I will perhaps one day sit down and hash through the `AccountController`, but needless to say, there's *some* amount of work to be done! I, for one, would like to see more best practices in place, a more referencable example of how to do things and sample views that better embrace the Bootstrap visuals (since, after all, it's included by default in the template).

Now on our end, we've done some off-script things as well, namely putting direct database access in a controller (and filter), pushing database models directly up to the view and leaning on those `ViewBag` properties to shuffle data around. So, yes, kettle, meet teapot.

All of these things are leading up to another set of writings on best practices 😄.

Chapter 27 Summary

It's rewarding to get to a point in your career where you get to use what you already know and take it up a level, rather than having to throw away the ways that get your work done. In this chapter we looked at how using the HTML skills you already have with the Bootstrap library can take a basic building block of any data-driven web site - the table - and make it look a lot more like 2014.

Following the existing conventions in the controller we used the `ViewBag` to push notifications to a view. We updated our markup that renders the tabs to include the partial view we created to display the notifications. Finally, we looked at the opportunities that exist in the default implementation of the `AccountController` to learn from and even avoid in our own works.

VI Wrapping Up With Some More Bootstrap

28. Doing More Interesting Things With Buttons

Using the styling of Bootstrap or a replacement theme is a great way to make your site stand out, and buttons are a great example of making the UI more rich and friendly to users. They are likely the first thing you'd write some CSS for if you were starting from scratch on your site, so the tweaks and highlights they offer out-of-box are quite welcome.

 Estimated time: Less than 25 minutes - settle in!

Basic Buttons

If you don't style your buttons, they're going to kinda suck. Well...it's not that they won't work or anything, but you will just get the boring old browser-styled version of a button.

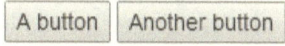

Boo...browser buttons!

And because each browser has it's own default stylesheet, you can't be guaranteed that any user will see the same font, layout or spacing. Thankfully, enforcing these attributes across clients is only an attribute away.

```
1   <button type="button" class="btn btn-primary btn-\
2   sm">A button</button>
3   <button type="button" class="btn btn-success btn-\
4   sm">Another button</button>
```

You'll notice that I used the btn-sm class in the source above, there are large (btn-lg), regular (no class needed), small (btn-sm) and extra-small (btn-xs) to choose from. And now my buttons look like so, in every browser:

Nearly pixel-perfect in every browser.

If I want them to be the same width, I can also use the grid system for sizing, dropping, say, a col-md-4 into the class attribute to get the following result:

Setting the width on buttons

Grouping Things Together

The buttons look better now, but they're bumping up against each other. They'd look better still if they looked like they were part of the same control group. We can assemble buttons into groups by providing a touch more markup to the elements, as seen below, with a simple DIV wrapper.

```
1  <div class="btn-group">
2      <!-- buttons here -->
3  </div>
```

Buttons grouped up for action

I changed the text here because this is the code that I'll be working into my partial for the notifications. I also made the buttons the same color – from a design stand point I think it looks better (and, heck, I'm even color blind) – and I removed the grid sizing on the buttons to allow them to group properly without having to add custom CSS styles.

Putting Some Fancy On

Chances are we could get away here with the two buttons side-by-each, but in the event that we need to add more actions the page is going to start to get a little wide. An improvement we can make here is to give the users a default action, but then to put the rest of the less-commonly accessed actions into a dropdown to look like this:

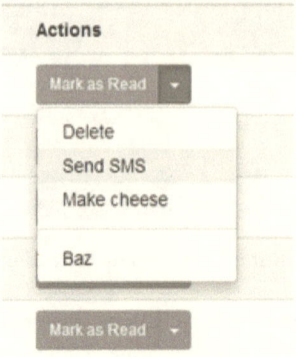

Dropdown-a-licious

This is called a split button dropdown, where a clickable action is available and additional commands are tucked into the drop down. Rather than wrapping the buttons in just a DIV, we also introduce a caret for the dropdown and have a UL/LI to act as a container for the non-visible actions.

```
1   <div class="btn-group">
2       <button type="button" class="btn btn-success \
3   btn-sm">Mark as Read</button>
4       <button type="button" class="btn btn-success \
5   btn-sm dropdown-toggle" data-toggle="dropdown">
6           <span class="caret"></span>
7           <span class="sr-only">Toggle Dropdown</sp\
8   an>
9       </button>
10      <ul class="dropdown-menu" role="menu">
11          <li><a href="#">Delete</a></li>
12          <li><a href="#">Send SMS</a></li>
13          <li><a href="#">Make cheese</a></li>
14          <li class="divider"></li>
15          <li><a href="#">Baz</a></li>
```

```
16      </ul>
17    </div>
```

I've added in the correct attributes on the caret button element – namely the data toggle – so that it plays properly with the framework. Per the documentation[1], I've also added an sr-only class that allows screen readers to make sense of the control grouping. The inner commands are now simply anchor tags and don't require any of the button classes.

So, there all-of-a-sudden seems to be a lot going on there, but let's break down the basic structure:

- A DIV to group everything together
- A BUTTON for the main action
- A BUTTON for the caret (dropdown)
- A UL with a list of LIs for the additional commands.

The skeleton looks like this:

```
1    <div class="btn-group">
2        <button type="button" class="btn">Primary Act\
3    ion</button>
4        <button type="button" class="btn dropdown-tog\
5    gle" data-toggle="dropdown">
6            <span class="caret"></span>
7            <span class="sr-only">Toggle Dropdown</sp\
8    an>
9        </button>
10       <ul class="dropdown-menu" role="menu">
11           <li><a href="#">...</a></li>
12           <li><a href="#">...</a></li>
13       </ul>
14   </div>
```

---

[1]http://getbootstrap.com/getting-started/#accessibility

One additional note: You would correctly assume, were you the assuming type, that the drop down functionality requires the JS library to work (which is already included in our web site bundle and layout).

Updating our View

Now, forget what we've done so far in the TD for our actions. We're going to change it up a bit and get things properly in line for some real-world action.

Since we're going to be changing data we are going to want to do a POST back to the server, so we have the option of using the Html.BeginForm helper. But generating a series of forms representing all actions for all notifications could get complicated quite quickly (in other words, we don't want a form for each action, for each notification).

Instead, we need to decorate our split buttons with the appropriate IDs, then put together a bit of JavaScript to do the submit for us on a single, static form. The form contains a hidden input for the ID and will be at the end of the document in _RenderNotifications, followed by the related JavaScript:

```
 1  <form id="notificationForm" method="POST"><input \
 2  type="hidden" name="id" id="notificationFormItemI\
 3  d" /></form>
 4
 5  <script type="text/javascript">
 6
 7      var readUrl = '@Url.Action("MarkNotificationA\
 8  sRead")';
 9      var deleteUrl = '@Url.Action("Delete")';
10
11      function updateNotification(id, action) {
```

```
12          $("#notificationFormItemId").val(id);
13          switch (action) {
14              case 'read':
15                  $("#notificationForm").attr('acti\
16  on', readUrl).submit();
17                  break;
18              case 'delete':
19                  $("#notificationForm").attr('acti\
20  on', deleteUrl).submit();
21                  break;
22              default:
23                  console.debug('Unknown action ' +\
24    action);
25          }
26      }
27
28  </script>
```

Here we are using the URL object's static helper method to resolve the URLs needed for read and delete actions. The JavaScript simply accepts the ID and an action parameter, then sets up the form correctly and submits it.

Next, skip back up the document a little to the TD that contains our split button. We'll replace the entire contents of the TD with the following:

```
1   <div class="btn-group">
2       <a class="btn btn-success btn-sm" href="javas\
3   cript:updateNotification(@notification.Notificati\
4   onId, 'read')">Mark as Read</a>
5       <button type="button" class="btn btn-success \
6   btn-sm dropdown-toggle" data-toggle="dropdown">
7           <span class="caret"></span>
8           <span class="sr-only">Toggle Dropdown</sp\
9   an>
10      </button>
11      <ul class="dropdown-menu" role="menu">
12          <li>
13              <a href="javascript:updateNotificatio\
14  n(@notification.NotificationId, 'delete')">Delete\
15  </a>
16          </li>
17          <li><a href="#">Send SMS</a></li>
18          <li><a href="#">Make cheese</a></li>
19          <li class="divider"></li>
20          <li><a href="#">Baz</a></li>
21      </ul>
22  </div>
```

You'll notice that our A tags are now just invoking our JavaScript method, passing in the notification ID of the current record (remember that we're in that outer foreach loop here). We can continue to develop new methods by wiring up the A tag and extending the switch statement should we like.

A Couple of Controller Methods

Finally we're going to need to wire up our controller to catch those user actions and do the dirty bits. Marking the notification as viewed will be first. We'll use the DB context to retrieve, update and save the selected record, so we'll make a small change to the way we initiate the DB context and move it to a class-level declaration as such:

```
1  private readonly SiteDataContext _context = new S\
2  iteDataContext();
```

Remember to remove the line of code from the GetUserNotifications method that was creating the context, and update the context variable to _context (your code won't compile if you don't).

Next, add the actions related to the commands we added to the page.

```
1  [HttpPost]
2  public ActionResult MarkNotificationAsRead(int id)
3  {
4      var userNotification = GetUserNotifications()\
5  .FirstOrDefault(n=>n.NotificationId == id);
6
7      if (userNotification == null)
8      {
9          return new HttpNotFoundResult();
10     }
11
12     userNotification.IsDismissed = true;
13     _context.SaveChanges();
14
15     return RedirectToAction("Manage");
16 }
```

Similarly, the code for the delete action will use the same DB context to delete the requested record.

```
1   [HttpPost]
2   public ActionResult Delete(int id)
3   {
4       var userNotification = GetUserNotifications()\
5   .FirstOrDefault(n => n.NotificationId == id);
6
7       if (userNotification == null)
8       {
9           return new HttpNotFoundResult();
10      }
11
12      _context.Notifications.Remove(userNotificatio\
13  n);
14      _context.SaveChanges();
15
16      return RedirectToAction("Manage");
17  }
```

There are a couple of quick notes here that I should mention. From a security standpoint we're doing some good things, namely, we're using a common method to only load into scope the notifications of the currently logged in user. We're leveraging the fact that the framework provides a mechanism to correctly provide the user's identity and limiting the user's request to only allow execution of modifying or deleting records in a "row-level" security kind of way. Our controller is marked with the Authorize attribute, so if we stack these altogether with SSL we'd be in pretty good shape.

Then there's the bits that aren't really good practice, but are good enough for the point of this exercise. First, we've got this GetUserNotifications method on the AccountController class. What about "AccountController" says anything about "loading the notifications for a specific user"? Nothing, right? This data access, as I've mentioned before, should be pushed into a repository that makes use of the DB context through a Dependency Injection mechanism that only creates one instance of the DB context per request. And, the controller should take that repository through DI. This would make things more flexible (why write data access in more than one spot) and testable (we could use mocks to test more easily).

Chapter 28 Summary

After adding the notifications to the Manage view in our project, the next obvious step was giving the users the ability to do something with them. In this chapter we looked at a few alternate ways that we can use buttons and their required element constructs. To tie those buttons to actual commands we also added a bit of JavaScript to handle the click events, and we wired up our controller actions to process the request with the introduction of the `MarkNotificationAsRead` and `Delete` methods.

29. Confirmation Dialogs for Delete Actions

We just gave our users the ability to delete a record from the database in the last chapter, but a single click does the deed without confirmation. It would likely be better to at least give them a little prompt to confirm that this is what they were trying to do in the first place.

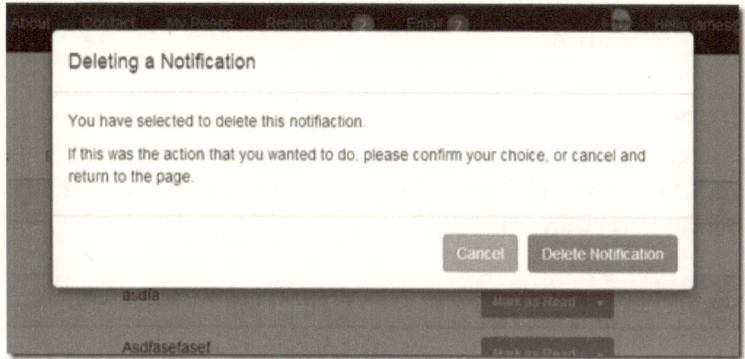

Confirming operations with modals

Let's first talk about how dialogs are composed and how to display them in a page.

 Estimated time: About 20 minutes

Bootstrap Modal Dialogs

Modals are made up of a wrapper, an outer and inner container and three common sections that provide default styling and handle proper rendering: the header, the body and the footer. You can represent the basic structure of the modal as follows:

```
1  <div class="modal">
2      <div class="modal-dialog">
3          <div class="modal-content">
4              <div class="modal-header">...</div>
5              <div class="modal-body">...</div>
6              <div class="modal-footer">...</div>
7          </div>
8      </div>
9  </div>
```

You can show a dialog by using a button with an attribute that Bootstrap is aware of:

```
1  <button class="btn" data-toggle="modal" data-targ\
2  et="#theModal">
3    Show my modal
4  </button>
```

Or you can invoke the modal by calling it from JavaScript:

```
1  $('#deleteConfirmModal').modal('show');
```

 For other events, defaults and other JavaScript method calls that are available, be sure to check out the docs on the Bootstrap site[1].

---

[1]http://getbootstrap.com/javascript/#modals

One thing that I've run into when using the button approach is the need to have the CSS selector on the data-target attribute (see the code above). I'm not sure why this is the approach, but if you forget that you need the hashtag as a prefix to the ID, your modal won't display. Regardless, we're going to be using JavaScript to do our work today, but keep that tip in mind as you start working with this on your own.

When using modals you'll want as little interference as possible with the styles and layout of the elements being used, so the recommendation is to put the container for the modal as close to the root of the document structure as possible.

The Game Plan

For this exercise we're going to hit a couple of areas of the project, so here's a quick checklist if you want to follow along. We're going to:

- Clean up our JavaScript and put it in a separate file
- Add an optionally rendered section to our _Layout page
- Add a partial view for the markup needed for our dialog
- Update the Manage view to include our new bits

Some Cleanup, Some JavaScript

We're going to start growing our client-side scripts on the view that renders notifications a little and one thing I like to do is to keep those bits organized. The JavaScript we have so far to give some UX for notifications is in our _RenderNotifications partial view, which presents some limitations as to when script can execute and whether or not jQuery has been loaded.

One easy way to keep these things straight, and organized in our project, is to add a _***PartialViewName***.js.cshtml file to our project in the same folder as our view. We can then consider the JavaScript related to the view as another asset that needs to be loaded on the full view.

So let's do that. Add a new view to the Views\Account folder called _RenderNotificationsjs. If you use the scaffolding tools, you'll notice that you can't properly name it (it complains about invalid characters), so add it as I've shown, then rename it to _Render-Notifications.js.cshtml once the file is there. Next, remove the old JavaScript from the _RenderNotifications.cshtml and put it in the new .js.cshtml file.

```
 1  <script type="text/javascript">
 2
 3      var readUrl = '@Url.Action("MarkNotificationA\
 4  sRead")';
 5      var deleteUrl = '@Url.Action("Delete")';
 6      var currentNotificationId;
 7
 8      function updateNotification(id, action) {
 9          $("#notificationFormItemId").val(id);
10          switch (action) {
11          case 'read':
12              $("#notificationForm").attr('action',\
13   readUrl).submit();
14              break;
15          case 'delete':
16              $("#notificationForm").attr('action',\
17   deleteUrl).submit();
18              break;
19          default:
20              console.debug('Unknown action ' + act\
21  ion);
22          }
23      }
```

```
24
25     function confirmDelete(id) {
26         currentNotificationId = id;
27         $('#deleteConfirmModal').modal('show');
28     }
29
30     $(function() {
31         $("#deleteConfirmModal").on('click', "#de\
32 leteConfirm", function() {
33             updateNotification(currentNotificatio\
34 nId, 'delete');
35         });
36     });
37
38 </script>
```

Remember that .cshtml gives us a little more power than just a straight .js file. We can do things like interact with the ViewBag or the page Model, write code that is parsed by Razor and make use of Html helper methods, all of which can be quite handy.

There's not too much more going on here than there was before, except that now we capture the ID of the notification in our confirmDelete method, and we are wiring up a click handler for the modal dialog that we're going to implement.

One final thing to do on our partial is to update the Delete button (the A tag) to call our new JavaScript method as follows:

```
1 <a href="javascript:confirmDelete(@notification.N\
2 otificationId)">Delete</a>
```

Rendering at the Root Using Optional Sections in our Layout

Remember the note about keeping the modal as close to the document root as possible? Well, there's a problem there when we're down at the view or partial view layer, stuck inside our other "main content" area of the page. We're inside all these other containers already and we can't break out without a little help from the MVC Framework.

What we want to do is to add another optional section, much like the scripts section that comes in the stock template. We can call this topLevel for now, though you'd likely want it to be more meaningful in a real project. Add the following code to your _Layout file.

```
1   @RenderSection("topLevel", required: false)
```

It should appear right after the BODY tag, first thing in the document, like this.

```
<body>
    @RenderSection("topLevel", required: false)

    <>...</>
    <>...</>

    @Scripts.Render("~/bundles/jquery")
    @Scripts.Render("~/bundles/bootstrap")
    @RenderSection("scripts", required: false)
</body>
```

Adding a new, optional section to our layout

Now, whenever you have something that will be injected from a view into the page in this topLevel section, you will be able to put elements directly into the root of the document.

Create the Modal Partial

Next up, we're going to create a _RenderNotifications.Modal.cshtml
partial view that has the HTML for our modal in it. This will help to
keep our core view simple, and keep our related files together in our
project. The markup for the modal follows the same basic structure
I highlighted above and adds a few other elements to the mix.

```
1   <div class="modal fade" id="deleteConfirmModal" t\
2   abindex="-1" role="dialog" aria-labelledby="delet\
3   eLabel" aria-hidden="true">
4       <div class="modal-dialog">
5           <div class="modal-content">
6               <div class="modal-header">
7                   <h4 class="modal-title" id="delet\
8   eLabel">Deleting a Notification</h4>
9               </div>
10              <div class="modal-body">
11                  <p>You have selected to delete th\
12  is notification.</p>
13                  <p>
14                      If this was the action that y\
15  ou wanted to do,
16                      please confirm your choice, o\
17  r cancel and return
18                      to the page.
19                  </p>
20              </div>
21              <div class="modal-footer">
22                  <button type="button" class="btn \
23  btn-success" data-dismiss="modal">Cancel</button>
24                  <button type="button" class="btn \
25  btn-danger" id="deleteConfirm">Delete Notificatio\
26  n</button>
```

```
27              </div>
28           </div>
29        </div>
30    </div>
```

There's a class 'fade' in there that tells bootstrap to slide and fade the modal in from the top. There are a few ARIA attributes in there for accessibility. I've added a title to the header, content in the body and buttons to either dismiss the dialog (canceling the delete) or to confirm the operation when the user elects to delete the notification.

Perhaps the most interesting bit in there is the data-dismiss attribute on the cancel button, which tells Bootstrap that this dialog can be hidden when the button is clicked.

Updating Our View

Finally, we update our view, adding the modal to the page and including the JavaScript that we need to pull it all together.

At the bottom of Manage.cshtml in Views\Account we add the topLevel section to the view and in it we render the modal markup from the partial view we created.

```
1    @section topLevel{
2
3        @{ Html.RenderPartial("_RenderNotifications.M\
4    odal"); }
5
6    }
```

Immediately after that, we update our scripts section to include the JS we need and created above.

```
1  @section Scripts {
2
3      @Scripts.Render("~/bundles/jqueryval")
4      @{ Html.RenderPartial("_RenderNotifications.j\
5  s"); }
6
7  }
```

Because we've kept things fairly organized along the way, changes to our view are minimal but at the same time we're able to improve the user experience a fair bit. We've added an easy way to get content into the root of our document and simplified our partial views. And look...

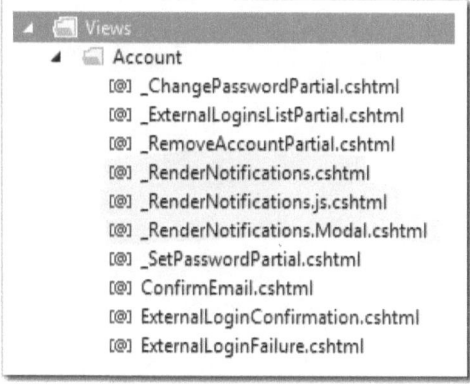

A fairly-organized Solution Explorer for all our component parts

...we even managed to keep our related files in one place in the solution explorer.

Our delete is now protected by the dialog, but we'd like to give the user a better picture of what it is they are deleting from the database. The generic dialog we are serving now is not enough to visually confirm the record that is being removed, particularly if our user happens to glance away from the page for a moment.

Chapter 29 Summary

We've continued to build on the real-world scenarios with appli-
cable components from the Bootstrap framework, and the addition
of a modal dialog is a much-needed utility in any UI toolbox. In
this chapter we learned about the markup required to put together
Bootstrap's version of a modal and fill it with content. We used the
MVC Framework to help us put content into the appropriate parts
of the DOM delivered to the client. We cleaned up some of our
files, adding new JavaScript and markup in a way that isn't overly
complicated to maintain.

30. Loading Bootstrap Modal Content via AJAX

Congrats! You've made it! Thirty chapters, maybe in thirty days, maybe even less. We still have one more loose end that I'd like to clean up, and we can reinforce some some of our AJAX knowledge in the process. Here we're going to revisit our modal dialog confirmation box that pops up when a user tries to delete a record and augment that experience. At this point, regardless of the notification selected for delete, the user will see the same static dialog. Let's improve upon that.

 Estimated time: Less than 20 minutes

Loading Remote Content With Bootstrap's Modal

There is built-in support for Bootstrap to load content into a modal, but there are some limitations. First, Bootstrap loads the content the first time the constructor is called on the modal. Secondly, the modal's constructor is only ever called once, meaning, you can't refresh the content without some extra script.

Rather than trying to put a square peg in a round hole, we can take the simpler approach of just loading the content with jQuery. After all, it's clean, easy to understand, and at the end of the day the modal is just HTML.

This approach will work better for us for the following use case:

- User selects to delete a notification
- They cancel out of the dialog
- The select a different notification to delete

At this point, the remote loading capabilities of Bootstrap's modal break down and we'd have to get into hacky stuff that may not survive a minor version upgrade. Pass! In my opinion, the modal should have an overload that accepts a 'remote URL' parameter.

If, however, you have a use case that doesn't involve refreshing the dialog, I encourage you to check out the docs[1] for using the built-in functionality.

Improving our Delete Confirmation

Rather than just giving a generic message, we're going to instead load some content via AJAX. This will give us a chance to put a visual preview of the data that will be deleted in front of the user.

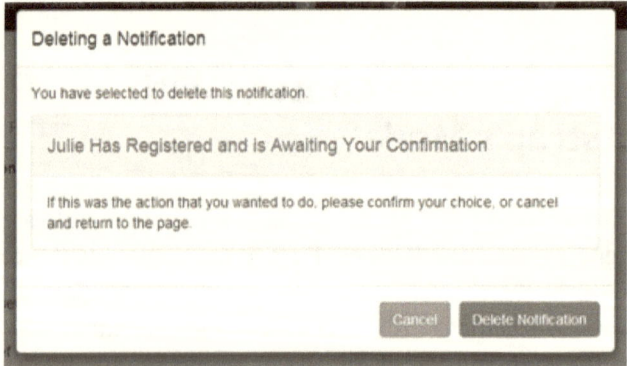

Confirming the record to delete in our modal

To accomplish this we're going to need to make small change to our modal markup (in Views\Account_RenderNotifications.Modal.cshtml), as follows:

---

[1]http://getbootstrap.com/javascript/#modals-usage

```
1  <div class="modal-body" id="notificationPreview">
2      <p>Loading content...</p>
3  </div>
```

What I've done here is removed the content from the modal-body section of the markup and replaced it with a loading message. I've also given the DIV an ID so that we can address it from JavaScript more directly. Also, revisit your Views\Account_RenderNotifications.js.cshtml and update the confirmDelete method, as we're now going to clear the contents and load the text dynamically.

```
1  function confirmDelete(id) {
2      currentNotificationId = id;
3      previewContainer.html('<p>Loading content...<\
4  /p>');
5      previewContainer.load(confirmUrl, { id: curre\
6  ntNotificationId });
7      $('#deleteConfirmModal').modal('show');
8  }
```

To pull that all together we need a couple more variable declarations at the top of the script. Here's my final list of vars:

```
1  var readUrl = '@Url.Action("MarkNotificationAsRea\
2  d")';
3  var deleteUrl = '@Url.Action("Delete")';
4  var confirmUrl = '@Url.Action("GetNotification")';
5  var previewContainer = $('#deleteConfirmModal #no\
6  tificationPreview');
7  var currentNotificationId;
```

You'll notice that I have added a confirm URL and captured the element (in previewContainer) that we are using for the confirm. This saves me from having to requery the DOM on each display of the dialog.

Adding the Controller Action

We're going to use that same pattern for loading up the notification
for the confirmation that we used for modifying and deleting. Let's
add a GetNotification method to our AccountController that has
the following code:

```
1  public ActionResult GetNotification(int id)
2  {
3      var userNotification = GetUserNotifications()\
4  .FirstOrDefault(n => n.NotificationId == id);
5
6      if (userNotification == null)
7      {
8          return new HttpNotFoundResult();
9      }
10
11     return PartialView("_RenderNotifications.Moda\
12  lPreview", userNotification);
13 }
```

This time, we'll be returning a partial view, as indicated in the code
above, that will help us render the relevant content for the user to
make their choice.

But hey...that code to load a single notification for the logged in
user is *crying* for some refactoring, am I right?

Adding the Partial View

The controller is wired to pass the single notification to a partial
view, which will essentially have the same information we had
in the content section of the modal markup, but now we'll also

render in some notification-specific information. You can use your imagination on how this could be further extended with more complex objects in your own project.

Here are the contents of _RenderNotifications.ModalPreview.cshtml, which you should put into Views\Account:

```
1   @model SimpleSite.Models.Notification
2
3   <p>You have selected to delete this notification.\
4   </p>
5   <p>
6       <div class="panel panel-warning">
7           <div class="panel-heading">
8               <h4>@Model.Title</h4>
9           </div>
10          <div class="panel-body">
11              If this was the action that you wante\
12  d to do,
13              please confirm your choice, or cancel\
14   and return
15              to the page.
16          </div>
17      </div>
18  </p>
```

Fire up the project and attempt to delete a notification to see this all in action.

Chapter 30 Summary - That's All Folks!

Well, there's a lot of moving parts now throughout the project, but if you've followed along you will have seen a lot of what Bootstrap has to offer and how you can make the most of that through the MVC Framework.

In this chapter we continued to improve our separation of concerns while improving the UI for our user. We added a placeholder to indicate that we were loading the record and an AJAX call that goes to fetch it. We took on the responsibility of loading the content ourselves to overcome some of the limitations of Bootstrap's default behavior. on the controller side, an action was put in place to retrieve the record from the database and render the partial view.

Wrapping it All Up

Thanks For Reading Along!

All things - good or bad - must come to an end. If you're reading this and feeling the "good" vibe, I hope that you recommend this book to friends and co-workers so that I can keep it up-to-date and in tune with future versions of MVC and Bootstrap. If you have that "not-so-good" vibe going, please *don't hesitate to reach out to me* so that I can improve things for future readers, or help you through any of your questions.

Both of these frameworks are here to stay. A solid commitment from Microsoft to continue building future versions of MVC has surfaced with exciting new features, configurability and run-time capabilities on the horizon. The inclusion of what is likely the world's most popular front-end framework in the MVC template is a further cue that we should be paying attention, especially since both of these foundations have left the doors open for us to extend and customize them as we see fit.

Hopefully these pages have helped move you along the path towards working with MVC and Bootstrap on a daily basis.

A Few Notes on our Project

Working through the exercises in this book will not land you with a starter project or a template to start building enterprise applications. In the grander scheme of things, I find it important to play with little bits that are easy to twiddle around and experiment, so I tried to present all of the content of this book in a way that lets you do the same.

Appendix I: Free Training For All the Peoples!

If this MVC thing is something that you are wanted to dive into more deeply, watching live speakers and getting to interact with experts is likely the next-best-thing to in-class training. If you can't make it to a conference or local user group, there plenty of options for you to invest some time in to hone your skills.

Microsoft Virtual Academy

There are two courses on MVA that were recorded somewhat in reverse order, but both featuring the same great presenters. I'll present them backwards here, as the more advanced session was recorded first.

Introduction to ASP.NET MVC

MVA - Intro to MVC

Join Jon Galloway and Christopher Harrison in live video training, for a hours of material on Microsoft Virtual Academy. This is free, people. Like breathing. You're getting top-quality information direct from the mothership, a real thorough examination of the basics of the MVC Framework. I had the wonderful privilege of joining Jon and Christopher behind the scenes, answering questions throughout the recording of the session. You'll even hear from me a little through the hosts!

> At time of publishing, this course is not yet available through MVA as on-demand content. I will update this chapter as soon as I am aware of availability here.

The ASP.NET MVC Framework

This was Jon and Christopher's first session, which was well received but generated demand for the introductory course. If you've already dabbled with MVC you can likely skip the intro and join the gents here. This course is a deep dive into the MVC internals, breaking down the pipeline, extension points and letting you get your hands dirty with some great content and sample code.

The course tells help to prepare you for Exam 70-486, important if you're seeking certification as an MCSD: Web.

Another easy one to lock in on, just stream the content[2] from the MVA site and bucket up to melt your mind.

---

[2]http://www.microsoftvirtualacademy.com/training-courses/developing-asp-net-mvc-4-web-applications-jump-start?prid=ca_mvpjc

Windows Azure Web Sites

If you're going to build an app, you're going to need somewhere to host it. Windows Azure provides many options for application development ranging from bare-metal VMs all the way up to application templates.

Join myself and Tejaswi Redkar as we explore options for building and deploying your next project.

Another free one, you can view the course here[3].

Online Resources

And, of course, there is always the interwebs! Here are some great resources that keep evolving the conversation around MVC and Bootstrap.

- The ASP.NET[4] website and MVC[5] sub-site
- The blogs of Jon Galloway[6], Scott Guthrie[7] and Scott Hanselman[8]
- Follow #aspnet[9] and #aspnetmvc[10] hash tags on twitter

And stay connected with *this guy right here* at my blog[11] and on Twitter as @CanadianJames[12].

[3]http://www.microsoftvirtualacademy.com/training-courses/windows-azure-web-sites-deep-dive-jump-start?prid=ca_mvpjc

[4]http://www.asp.net

[5]http://www.asp.net/mvc

[6]http://weblogs.asp.net/jongalloway

[7]http://weblogs.asp.net/scottgu

[8]http://www.hanselman.com/

[9]https://twitter.com/search?q=%23aspnet

[10]https://twitter.com/search?q=%23aspnetmvc

[11]http://jameschambers.com

[12]https://twitter.com/CanadianJames

Appendix II: The Frameworks Feature Guide

If you've read through the book and picked up on a few concepts that you'd like to revist, I've put together this index of sorts to let you jump quickly to the content you're looking for, organized by framework feature rather than as the progression that you walked through in the book.

Note that if you *haven't* followed along, all of this content is based on the linear continuation from chapters previous, so you can't jump into Chapter 29 without the work from earlier chapters. You can, however, get the code for the book and switch to the completed chapter branch in the repo to let you start working with the examples that were presented in each section. Just switch to that branch and you should be good to go.

Many of these topics you'll find scattered through the book, but I'll note below the most interesting aspects of each subject. Mostly, this guide will serve a reader who has completed the book and is looking to drill straight into something for reference or background.

The MVC Framework

- Controllers: 3, 4, 12, 18, 27
- Actions: 3, 12, 20, 28
- Views and Partials: 3, 4, 6, 12, 14, 22, 29
- Filters: 20, 21
- Layouts: 2, 6, 21, 29
- Security & Identity: 22, 24, 25, 29
- Execution Pipeline: 1, 14, 20
- Data & Model Binding: 11, 19, 24, 25

The Bootstrap Framework

- Grid System: 5
- Labels: 4, 6, 7, 8
- Badges: 18, 19, 20
- Checkboxes and Radio Buttons: 7, 8,
- Buttons: 4, 5, 7, 28
- Forms: 12, 13
- Tables: 15, 27
- Modals: 29, 30
- Customizing Bootstrap: 17, 18

Bootstrap *by @mdo*[13] *and @fat*[14] - http://getbootstrap.com/about/

The MVC Framework *by Microsoft* - http://www.asp.net/mvc

"Aldrin Apollo 11 original" *by NASA* - http://www.hq.nasa.gov/alsj/a11/AS11-40-5903HR.jpg. Licensed under Public domain via Wikimedia Commons - http://commons.wikimedia.org/wiki/File:Aldrin_Apollo*11_-original.jpg#mediaviewer/File:Aldrin_Apollo*11_original.jpg

---

[13]https://twitter.com/mdo
[14]https://twitter.com/fat